THE

HEALTH GUIDE TO

ADULT BIPOLAR DISORDER
2ND EDITION

Dear Reader,

No one who develops a mental disorder is at fault; the cause lies somewhere in the interaction of genes and environment. Bipolar and other disorders have a biological basis, just as any disease that affects other organs in the body.

Emma Parker Bowles suffered from bipolar disorder for years. After she found help and effective treatment, she wrote in an essay, "I know I am not the only one. So if reading this helps just one person not to feel so alone, not to feel so lost in the fog, then it was worth it. Just don't suffer in silence. Don't be ashamed. Talk about it. Explore treatment options and find something that will work for you. I leave you with this African proverb: 'However long the night, the dawn will break.'"

Picking up a book such as this one is a good first step to learning about the nature of this disease and what you can do about it. If you arm yourself with as much knowledge as you can gather from this and other books, medical authorities, support groups, and people who have bipolar disorder, you will shorten the night.

Dean A. Haycock, PhD

WELCOME TO THE

EVERYTHING®

HEALTH GUIDES

Everything® Health Guides are a part of the bestselling *Everything®* series and cover important health topics like anxiety, postpartum care, and thyroid disease. Packed with the most recent, up-to-date data, *Everything®* Health Guides help you get the right diagnosis, choose the best doctor, and find the treatment options that work for you. With this one comprehensive resource, you and your family members have all the information you need right at your fingertips.

 Alerts

Urgent warnings

 Facts

Important snippets of information

 **Essentials**

Quick handy tips

 Questions

Answers to common questions

When you're done reading, you can finally say you know **EVERYTHING®**!

PUBLISHER Karen Cooper

DIRECTOR OF ACQUISITIONS AND INNOVATION Paula Munier

MANAGING EDITOR, EVERYTHING® SERIES Lisa Laing

COPY CHIEF Casey Ebert

ACQUISITIONS EDITOR Katrina Schroeder

ASSOCIATE DEVELOPMENT EDITOR Hillary Thompson

EDITORIAL ASSISTANT Ross Weisman

EVERYTHING® SERIES COVER DESIGNER Erin Alexander

LAYOUT DESIGNERS Colleen Cunningham, Elisabeth Lariviere, Ashley Vierra, Denise Wallace

Visit the entire Everything® series at *www.everything.com*

THE

EVERYTHING®

HEALTH GUIDE TO

ADULT BIPOLAR DISORDER

2ND EDITION

A reassuring guide for patients
and families

Dean A. Haycock, PhD
Foreword by Sheldon Whitten-Vile, MD

Avon, Massachusetts

For Marie E. Culver and Florence Moratelli

An Everything® Series Book.
Everything® and everything.com® are registered trademarks of F+W Media, Inc.

Published by Adams Media, a division of F+W Media, Inc.
57 Littlefield Street, Avon, MA 02322 U.S.A.
www.adamsmedia.com

ISBN 10: 1-4405-0405-9
ISBN 13: 978-1-4405-0405-1
eISBN 10: 1-4405-0406-7
eISBN 13: 978-1-4405-0406-8

Printed in the United States of America.

10 9 8 7 6 5 4 3 2 1

Library of Congress Cataloging-in-Publication Data
is available from the publisher.

Many of the designations used by manufacturers and sellers to distinguish their products are claimed as trademarks. Where those designations appear in this book and Adams Media was aware of a trademark claim, the designations have been printed with initial capital letters.

This book is intended as general information only, and should not be used to diagnose or treat any health condition. In light of the complex, individual, and specific nature of health problems, this book is not intended to replace professional medical advice. The ideas procedures and suggestions in this book are intended to supplement, not replace, the advice of a trained medical professional. Consult your physician before adopting any of the suggestions in this book, as well as about any condition that may require diagnosis or medical attention. The author and publisher disclaim any liability arising directly or indirectly from the use of this book.

*This book is available at quantity discounts for bulk purchases.
For information, please call 1-800-289-0963.*

Acknowledgments

This is the second Everything® book I have done for Adams Media, and Katrina Schroeder edited both of them. She is a pleasure to work with. This book is a revision of the first edition written by Jon P. Block, PhD. I had permission to keep as much of his material in the book as I wanted. In many cases, I have done so where new developments have not made it necessary to change his material. I acknowledge his influence and contributions, which can be found in this revision. As always, I am grateful to Marie E. Culver, who should know what Everything means to an author.

Contents

Foreword

Psychiatry is one of medicine's most misunderstood disciplines. Despite frequent portrayals in the popular media, bipolar affective disorder (manic depression) remains one of psychiatry's most misunderstood diagnoses. Many who suffer from this illness believe they don't have it, and there are some who are certain they have it, but don't. Unfortunately, psychiatrists tend to see more of the former, and persuading people, especially young people, that they have a serious mental illness is extremely difficult. While depressed people often know they have a problem, and are often willing to seek treatment, most manic individuals do not see a problem or a need for help. They often put themselves and their loved ones through a number of horrific episodes before they "get it." What makes this even more tragic is that good, effective treatments are available, and most people with this illness can live a "normal" life if they find, and stick with, appropriate treatment.

For those people who wonder if they have bipolar disorder, there is little awareness of the variety of alternative diagnoses that may be more accurate. The right diagnosis is the first step in getting the right treatment.

Psychoeducation is the education offered to people who live with psychological disturbances. Its goal is to help the patient understand and be better able to deal with the illness. It also helps to reinforce the patient's own strengths, resources, and coping skills, so they can become active participants in their health and well-being.

In addition, friends and family members are frequently confused about what is happening to their loved ones. Often, the normal, supportive responses are not helpful, and families are afraid to say or do "the wrong thing" and potentially make things worse. They wonder what went wrong, what they can do to help, and what the future holds for the patient.

I spend a considerable part of my time trying to educate patients and family members about bipolar affective disorder. Many patients and family members ask where they can look for more information, and bemoan the absence of a book such as this one. This book fills a valuable need in explaining to the average person what bipolar disorder is and how to deal with it.

Dr. Haycock has done a masterful job of explaining a complex subject in a way anyone can understand. In clear, easy to understand language, he describes the symptoms, goes through the history, causes, treatments, and explains living with this disorder. There are many complicating factors in the diagnosis and treatment of bipolar disorder. This includes the effect on the family, misdiagnoses and alternative diagnoses, substance abuse, creativity, medications, and alternative treatments. He addresses just about every possible concern that someone with this illness, or whose loved one suffers from this illness, might have.

I expect this book to be the first choice of general physicians, psychiatrists, psychologists, social workers, and therapists for bipolar disorder patients and their families. This book is not only an indispensable source of information, but may be used as a valuable adjunct to the therapeutic process.

—Sheldon Whitten-Vile, MD

Introduction

Bipolar disorder has been called the medical condition du jour. For some people, it is mistakenly seen as a trendy disorder associated with artists, writers, actors, and creative high achievers. It has been linked to many celebrities, who have talked about their struggle with the disorder. In so doing, these well-known spokespersons have performed an admirable service by helping remove the stigma associated with mental disorders of all types.

But a few people reason that if famous, accomplished people have bipolar disorder, it might not be such a bad thing to have. This naïve view is never shared by anyone who has suffered from this illness. Untreated, it can be life threatening: suicide claims 15 percent or more of those who struggle with this brain disease.

Despite the increased public awareness of the disorder, the common belief around the world that a mental disorder is a source of embarrassment—a personal flaw—persists. The masses of people who aren't writers, artists, or entertainers, who don't have publicists but do have bipolar disorder—and there are millions of them—don't see glamour in the illness. Instead, they experience disrupted lives, personal pain, and often discrimination.

Faced with the reality of their diagnosis, they recover their health by taking charge and managing their illness. They learn to recognize their symptoms, intercept destructive mood swings, and continue their treatment. The odds are in your favor if you do the same.

CHAPTER 1

The Basics of Bipolar Disorder

The term bipolar disorder refers to a group of brain diseases that cause moods to fluctuate widely and uncontrollably. It can cause you to move from depression to mania, from spirit-crushing and potentially life-threatening lows to dangerous highs. These extreme fluctuations have a negative impact on a person's energy level, thoughts, behavior, and ability to function. Although not curable, bipolar disorder can be controlled with treatment. It is difficult to determine precisely how many people have this disorder, but the National Institute of Mental Health estimates that approximately 5.7 million adults are dealing with it in the U.S. This means two or three out of every 100 adults in the U.S. has some form of bipolar disorder. Half of them are over twenty-five years of age when they develop the disease. Worldwide, more than 250 million people may have bipolar disorder.

What Is Bipolar Disorder?

Bipolar disorder is one of four major mood disorders recognized by psychiatrists. The others are unipolar depression and mood disorders induced by substances or due to a general medical condition. Once called manic-depression or manic-depressive illness, bipolar disorder is a serious medical condition whose recurring episodes of mania and major depression distinguish it not only from normal mood fluctuations but from other mood disorders as well. The extremes in mood swings—unless treated—can seriously affect well-being by damaging relationships, sabotaging educations and careers, and threatening financial security and personal safety.

Like many complex mental disorders, bipolar disorder cannot be cured, but it can be effectively treated with medication, therapy, and healthy lifestyle choices. There may be a long delay—lasting years in many cases—between the first appearance of symptoms and diagnosis and treatment. The disorder can be difficult to diagnose because the symptoms vary with time. Often, it is confused with depression. Other symptoms of bipolar disorder, considered in isolation, can lead to misdiagnoses. Only when the complete picture of bipolar symptoms are inventoried and considered is an accurate diagnosis possible. Once correctly identified and treated, however, experience has shown that you can live a rewarding, productive life free from the debilitating, extreme fluctuation of severe depression and mania.

Manic Episodes

Some people think that having lots of energy and enthusiasm is the same as experiencing a manic state. It's not. There are easy ways to tell the difference.

Rapid Speech, High Energy, and Euphoria

Mania involves lightning-quick ideas that people barely have time to process or verbalize. This nevertheless does not stop them from trying, and they may talk nonstop. Speech may even become nonsensical with rhyming of words for no reason or making illogical or disconnected observations. Words may come so quickly that a listener can't follow them and the speaker can become hoarse from trying to keep up with his thoughts.

Another common symptom is seemingly boundless energy. Someone experiencing mania might go for days without sleep. They may exhibit a childlike blend of fascination and impatience toward different activities or people. Like a child quickly engaged—and just as quickly bored—someone in a manic phase often flits from one pursuit to the next, from one unrealistic plan to another one.

Essential

Bipolar disorder can play a role in serious crimes. Recent studies suggest significant connections between bipolar disorder and spousal and child abuse. Mania can inspire people to commit acts of larceny, extortion, or fraud. In *The Informant!*, a movie based on a nonfiction book, the character played by actor Matt Damon is said to have bipolar disorder, which contributed to embezzling activity that resulted in prosecution and jail time.

Mania can be characterized by a strong sense of euphoria, but this euphoria can switch to anger or hostility very quickly. Someone who seems deliriously happy one moment can become irritated in an instant, for example.

Manic Thinking, Manic Psychosis

Manic episodes also may involve grandiosity resulting in the belief that you are much more accomplished, brilliant, talented, inventive, beautiful, etc. than you really are. The slightest accomplishment can be elevated to an outlandish degree. A routine task such as taking out the trash, for example, might be described as profound an experience as curing cancer. You may develop an unrealistically high level of self-confidence and dangerous optimism. In your eyes, you may become great, and believe nothing bad could happen to you. Insight and self-reflection fade. It can be extremely difficult to convince someone experiencing mania that something is not right and that he should seek help.

In extreme cases, manic thinking can become manic psychosis, in which a person hallucinates or hears voices that support his grandiose view of himself. Common delusions include having extraordinary talent or skill or being rich or aristocratic. Or a person might believe he can heal the sick with his touch. Delusions can also inspire feelings of persecution.

Risk Taking, Sex, and Nosiness

Mania is often associated with risk-taking behavior. This can include: sudden and unplanned trips, business investments, and spur-of-the-moment marriages; compulsive gambling; giving away possessions or paying people's bills; running up huge phone bills; buying expensive cars, jewelry, or large quantities of less expensive items; and calling attention to oneself in public by shouting, preaching, dancing, or singing in the street.

Another symptom of mania is increased sexual activity. A person with bipolar disorder might become involved with a casual acquaintance or stranger to satisfy a sudden and intense sexual need. It is not uncommon for someone with years of untreated bipolar disorder to have a long list of marriages and/or people with whom she has had sexual contact.

 Fact

Jayson Blair's career as a *New York Times* reporter ended in 2003 because he copied stories from other newspapers and fabricated quotes and sources. Grandiosity, inflated self-esteem, and high-risk behavior all seem to have played a role in his unfortunate self-destruction as a journalist. Since then, Blair has become a certified life coach, using his "experience with bipolar disorder and other issues to help others in similar situations," according to his website.

Another common symptom of a manic episode is inappropriate involvement in other people's lives—being a super-busybody. A person with the disorder may make, without invitation, others' personal or professional matters her own business. She might make phone calls at inappropriate times, offer long-winded and unsolicited advice, or make bullying threats. Friends and family often distance themselves to escape this meddlesome, boorish behavior.

Manic episodes can require hospitalization, for the safety of both the patient and those around him. Untreated, it can have tragic consequences.

Depressive Episodes

The depression experienced by a person with bipolar disorder is, as the name suggests, the polar opposite of mania—and can be even more dangerous. The senses, except emotional pain, seem to shut down during such depressions. Initiative, interest, and joy evaporate. Instead of feeling grandiose, a person in a depressive state may feel guilty and worthless and think of suicide. Being alive literally becomes painful for a severely depressed person.

Reverse of Mania

Eating and sleeping patterns during depression may be the reverse of those during mania. If someone in a manic state could not slow down to eat, he may become ravenously hungry in a depressed state or, if he took great pleasure in eating in the manic state, he may have little appetite when depressed. Rather than having so much energy that he can go without sleep, a person suffering through a depressed stage of bipolar disorder now appears to have no energy at all and may want to do little besides sleep. Also, it is not uncommon for people in a depressed state to complain of physical aches and pains that have no physiological cause.

During an episode of depression, activities that used to engage a person no longer do. It becomes hard to concentrate on anything; gone is the intense (if fleeting) interest common in manic episodes. A person with depression loses interest in people he formerly cared about. He becomes reclusive, turning down social invitations, preferring solitude.

Depression causes a person to feel defeated; nothing seems worth trying. Someone in this state has difficulty making decisions about even the smallest things.

L. Essential

One feature of manic episodes is accelerated psychomotor activity. This means there is an increase in bodily activity: pacing, walking, fidgeting, gesturing. In contrast, depressive episodes are typified by psychomotor retardation. Body movement is less rapid and active, due to diminished mental activity.

Like manic episodes, depression can involve anger and irritability, but this does not fluctuate with euphoria; instead, it fluctuates with anxiety, fear, and agitation. A person with bipolar disorder might cry for long periods. Even when not crying, a person suffering through a depressed stage of bipolar disorder conveys grave sadness and a sense of despair.

At its most extreme, a depressive episode can lead to thoughts of suicide. Living seems to be such a painful burden and a person's life seems to her so unworthy that dying seems to offer the only relief. (See Chapter 8.)

Even short of a suicide attempt, the depression associated with this and other mood disorders may cause someone to develop a strong attraction to matters pertaining to death. Ironically, it might be the one topic that sparks his interest. In fact, seriously depressed people can seem strangely energized before taking their own lives. Family, friends, coworkers, and acquaintances might even think that the person was "getting better" or "snapping out of it." They report being shocked to learn that the person committed suicide. Relief that their emotional pain will soon end may account for the apparent improved moods sometimes observed in depressed patients who have decided to end their lives.

The History of the Disorder

One of the earliest descriptions of what is now called bipolar disorder appeared in the writings of the Greek physician Aretaeus of Cappadociam in the second century A.D. He noted the existence of both manic and depressive moods in the same individuals. It took more than 1,000 years before his basic observations were extended in 1650 by the British writer Richard Burton. Burton wrote a landmark volume entitled *The Anatomy of Melancholia*. Burton focused on melancholia, or what we now call depression, and some of his insights on depression are still employed today. Burton's relevance to bipolar disorder, however, stems from his description of symptoms in terms of their relative "melancholia"; his influential book tends to underemphasize the role of mania in this type of mood disorder.

 Fact

"Manic depression" is an older term, but even in some current literature it is used interchangeably with bipolar disorder. Some experts feel it is a better name for the condition than bipolar disorder. If you are shopping for information on bipolar disorder and are uncertain about a source that calls it manic depression, check the publication date. If it has been published within the past ten years, you might consider it relatively up to date, but not necessarily. Date of publication alone, of course, is no guarantee of reliability. Check the qualifications of the source of the information you consult.

Bipolar disorder was described as an illness in its own right by two nineteenth-century French doctors, Jean Falret and Jules Baillarger. Working independently in the 1850s, they distinguished what they called *folie circulaire* (circular insanity) or *folie à double forme* (dual-form insanity) from simple depression and full-blown mania without depression. (The word "insanity" is not part of current medical terminology, although it still has meaning in legal proceedings and, of course, in popular culture.)

It was not until the early 1900s that the German psychiatrist Emil Krapelin presented his concept of "manic depressive insanity" and introduced the term into medical terminology. Krapelin's ideas on manic depression were accepted slowly, but eventually widely, by the medical community.

In the 1950s and 1960s, psychiatrists re-evaluated features of unipolar (depression) and bipolar (mania and depression) mood disorders. They looked at what was then known about genetics, gender, age of onset, and symptoms that distinguished the two conditions.

Three researchers, Carlo Perris, Jules Angst, and George Winoku, working independently during the 1960s, published works that influenced our present acceptance of the existence of bipolar disorders. They helped to clearly demonstrate the differences between unipolar and bipolar disorders.

This and other research led to the 1980 decision by the American Psychiatric Association to refer to the body of symptoms as "bipolar disorder" in the third edition of its official *Diagnostic and Statistical Manual of Mental Disorders*. (The current edition, DSM IV, was published in 2000. The fifth edition, DSM V, is scheduled to be released in 2013.)

Major Types of Bipolar Disorder

There are three basic subtypes of bipolar disorder: bipolar I, bipolar II, and cyclothymia. Subclassifications of these three help psychiatrists refine their diagnoses. A major difference between the main subdivisions of bipolar disorder is the degree or severity of the symptoms. Bipolar I involves periods of extreme mania, often with alternating episodes of depression. Bipolar II involves periods of less extreme mania alternating with episodes of depression. Cyclothymia entails frequent periods of depression and less severe mania; symptoms are milder than in other types of the disorder.

Bipolar I

Bipolar I is the most serious form of the illness. One of its key features is the occurrence of at least one manic or one mixed episode. It is also possible that you may, but not necessarily, have experienced a major depressive episode in the past. Many people with bipolar I have had episodes of serious depression before being diagnosed.

Sometimes both mania and depression are present at more or less the same time, but the emphasis may be somewhat more on mania. You may experience several manic episodes and/or manic-depressive episodes and then a depressive one.

Mania can fuel intense anger or mistrust and can result in spontaneous harm to self or others. Here is how writer Marya Hornbacher, who endured years of torment including anorexia and substance abuse, recalls her rages: "It seemed to happen overnight: one day I am calm, and the next I am raging. It's very simple. Happens like you're flipping a switch. Julian [her husband] and I are going along, having a perfectly lovely evening, and then it's dark and I am screaming, standing in the middle of the room, turning over the glass-topped coffee table, ripping the bathroom sink out of the wall, picking up anything nearby and pitching it as hard as I can. The rages always come at night. They control my voice, my hands." Eventually, Hornbacher was diagnosed with bipolar I. She tells her story in her book *Madness, A Bipolar Life.*

While depression is more likely to lead to intentional suicide, it can also make a person feel so bad about life that out of "mercy" she decides to kill other people, including her own children. It is not difficult to see why it is essential that a person with Bipolar I seek treatment—if untreated, she will be lucky to be hospitalized before causing major harm.

Bipolar II

If you have bipolar II disorder, you have had at least one major depressive episode and at least one hypomanic episode. Hypomania is a less severe form of mania, and these episodes will tend to outnumber your depressed episodes. You will not have had a fully manic or a mixed episode, however. The disruption bipolar II produces in your life may be less than that caused by bipolar I; for example, you may have problems at work or with relationships, but you are still able to function reasonably well in other areas of your life.

 ## Question

> **What is Bipolar Spectrum Illness?**
> Symptoms such as changing moods, impulsive behavior, and irritability are not limited to bipolar disorder. Some psychiatrists who see them in patients with other disorders suspect that bipolar I and II are part of a spectrum that may include eating disorders, substance abuse, and recurrent major depressive disorder. Perhaps, they reason, some people with these disorders might respond to lithium or other medications used to treat bipolar disorder if they don't respond to antidepressants. The case for bipolar spectrum illness, however, needs more proof before it can be accepted by most psychiatrists.

While bipolar II is not as serious as bipolar I, it can be harder to detect. This can cause problems in several ways.

First, it often means the condition is not recognized for what it is. It might be mistaken for simple depression, leading to inappropriate treatment. It is important to understand that treatments for unipolar depression (depression without mania) are not the proper treatments for bipolar disorders. Next, there is a risk that improperly treated symptoms can escalate. While it is possible to stay at the bipolar II level indefinitely, it is also possible that your symptoms may worsen to the level of bipolar I. This transition is more likely over time as events take a toll and exacerbate the untreated symptoms.

Additionally, there is the matter of heightened depression. Since the intensity of depressive episodes is more intense than the intensity of hypomanic episodes, thoughts of death and suicide can pose a serious risk. The seemingly happy person who shocks family, friends, and coworkers by committing suicide might have been suffering from undiagnosed bipolar II.

Hypomania

The relatively minor manic episodes seen in bipolar II are called hypomania. It has many features in common with mania, but does not result in elevated moods as extreme as those seen in full-blown mania.

Instead of feeling euphoric, a person having a hypomanic episode experiences unrealistically heightened confidence. With hypomania, you might notice how assertive or outgoing you suddenly have become. You might find that you have the courage to do things you might have avoided before: ride a scary roller coaster, make a high dive into a pond, go parachuting or hang gliding, speak in public, or sing karaoke. You may feel oddly in tune with life and feel like you know exactly what to say or do.

 Fact

Normal and abnormal moods seem to lie on a continuous spectrum. At one extreme is severe mania. It blends into a less severe mania called hypomania. Hypomania is closer to a balanced or normal mood viewed as healthy. As moods pass to the opposite end of the spectrum, they become moderate depression and finally severe depression. This neat scheme is complicated a bit by the existence of mixed moods, which have symptoms of both depression and agitation.

You also are likely to engage in more sexual activity and thoughtless spending. Again, none of this is quite as extreme as with mania. For example, people experiencing hypomania might be more discreet in pursuing sex than if they suffered from mania. You may not spend all your money, but you may spend beyond what you can realistically and safely afford. And unlike mania, hypomania is not associated with full-blown psychosis.

In hypomania, people usually cannot do without sleep altogether, but they do sleep less. Their thoughts are not expressed as incoherently, in a nonstop stream, as they are during a period of mania, but they are heightened and more rapid than usual. People experiencing hypomania do not talk nonstop until they are hoarse, but they do talk more than usual. For example, people who normally do not interrupt others in conversation are suddenly unable to resist butting in.

Puzzling Mood Shifts

In hypomania, sudden confidence can vanish quickly. People who met you while you were outgoing, vocal, fun loving, and enthusiastic might be baffled at the relative level of social discomfort you display once your mood returns to "normal." On the other hand, people who have known you longer might wonder why you are suddenly not behaving like the person they thought they knew. People closest to you will notice a change.

Friends, coworkers, and family, as well as the patient, might be exasperated by the ebb and flow of confidence and drive associated with hypomania. An undiagnosed individual might wonder why he could not stand up to his boss on Friday when he had no trouble doing so on Monday. Over time, the cycle renders him increasingly confused about himself and apprehensive about his unexplainable personality shifts.

Concentration and Goals

Hypomania causes a person to become easily distracted and have difficulty concentrating, but the effect is not as dramatic as it is in full-scale mania. For example, rather than rapidly dropping complete interest in one activity or person for another, someone with hypomania might complain of having trouble concentrating on a project. During hypomania, a person might ask you to repeat several times what you just said because he was thinking of something else during the conversation.

If you have bipolar II, you might be obsessed with achieving a particular personal or professional goal. For example, you might turn down an invitation to go out to dinner because a work report "must" get finished, even though there is plenty of time to complete the report during normal working hours. In fact, you might end up spending little time that evening working on the task that prevented you from accepting the dinner invitation if other tasks distract you. Another manifestation of this type of behavior might be an intense focus upon trivial details, which take up much more time than they warrant. Thus, a five-page report might become a twenty-five page report. People who abuse diet pills and amphetamines sometimes experience this type of single-minded focus.

Dangers of Hypomania

Though more euphoric than someone's "normal" behavior, hypomanic episodes are less likely to signal that someone needs hospitalization or is otherwise in serious danger. In fact, some people might think being hypomanic isn't so bad. It has its obvious drawbacks, yet it also might sound attractive to feel highly confident or goal driven. It even sometimes passes for highly enthusiastic normal behavior.

Essential

If anyone suggests that employers should go out of their way to hire people with hypomania, they are missing some important points. This ironic reverse discrimination indicates that many people see only the superficial "up" side of hypomania, and not the inefficiency that often accompanies it, not to mention it's reverse side: depression. Furthermore, bipolar II symptoms can worsen to become bipolar I symptoms.

There is an ironic aspect of bipolar II: Since hypomania is less likely to cause serious problems in someone's everyday life, an individual may be misdiagnosed as simply depressed when that symptom becomes the dominant mood. The hypomanic state might be misinterpreted as evidence of enthusiasm; it might not be recognized as part of the problem. But it is extremely important to remember that hypomania is related to depression in bipolar II and is part of the same illness. Where there is hypomania, there will be depression.

Cyclothymia

The third form of bipolar disorder, cyclothymia or cyclothymic disorder, differs from the others in terms of the severity of its symptoms. If you have a basic familiarity of the manic, depressive, and hypomanic symptoms that distinguish bipolar I and bipolar II from normal mood changes, you already know some of the most important facts about this condition.

Distinct from Bipolar I and II

Cyclothymia is characterized by less intense cycles of both mania and depression. By contrast, bipolar II is milder only when it comes to mania; the depressive stage can be just as serious and debilitating as in bipolar I. Less intense, however, does not necessarily mean less threatening, since untreated cyclothymia can lead to full-blown bipolar disorder.

People with cyclothymia have periods of depression and hypomania. However, they don't have full-blown manic episodes, major depressive episodes, or mixed episodes (which combine features of both depression and mania). Symptoms have to have been around for at least two years and never absent for more than two months for a diagnosis of cyclothymia.

As with the hypomania associated with bipolar I, dramatic shifts in energy from high to low, unpredictable mood changes, marked changes in ability to concentrate or engage in introspection, and heightened or dulled perceptions are features of this form of bipolar disorder. Emotions are strong, and there may be a desire to shock or act in an outrageous manner. Unlike other forms of bipolar disorder, however, a patient may not have exceptionally powerful sexual urges. And although the depression is not as great as in bipolar I or II, someone with cyclothymia still feels quite down when the disorder shifts in that direction.

On balance, cyclothymia, though less dramatic than bipolar I or II, can have a significantly negative impact on the quality of a person's life. It must be treated, especially since it can progress to a more serious mood disorder.

Other Variations

Many mental disorders seem to lie on a spectrum in which symptoms can subtly blend and vary in degree. Some people develop clear and incapacitating symptoms, while others have less severe symptoms, combinations of symptoms, or a personality with traits that remind people of more serious problems. These variations of mental disorder may be related.

Classifying and Refining the Concept of Bipolar Disorder

Because patients are seen at different stages in the course of their illnesses and symptoms vary, psychiatrists have developed a variety of classifications to describe the different types of problems for which patients seek help. For example, someone might have bipolar I with a single manic episode.

Someone with recurring mood fluctuations might be described as having recurrent bipolar disorder with a recent episode of mania or hypomania. Other individuals might best be described as having recurrent bipolar I disorder with one of the following episodes: depressed, mixed, or even unspecified. In addition to bipolar I, II, and cyclothymia, doctors sometimes diagnose bipolar disorder NOS, or not otherwise specified, if they can't pin down a more specific diagnosis.

Mixed Episodes

Sometimes a person with bipolar I can have symptoms of mania and depression at the same time. Also known as depressed or dysphoric mania, this mixed state can cause a person to be irritable and short tempered. Negativity and hopelessness can combine with agitation. It might be difficult for some people not familiar with bipolar disorder to imagine, but being in a mixed state may mean feeling very sad or hopeless and highly energized at the same time. There is no euphoria as there is in mania; euphoria is replaced by agitation in a mixed episode.

Mixed episodes can be confusing to the onlooker who does not know someone's history of bipolar disorder. It is easy to lose patience with someone having a mixed episode, because it seems no matter what you say or do, it makes the person unhappy, and no matter how reassuring you are, you fail to reassure or calm her.

 Fact

On occasion, a patient has symptoms that look like bipolar disorder, yet don't seem to fit any of the known patterns. In these instances, she might be diagnosed as having bipolar disorder not otherwise specified, or bipolar NOS. This classification enables a doctor to classify the patient as bipolar and see how the illness is or is not being manifested according to established diagnostic guidelines. A formal classification is also required by insurance companies before they consider reimbursing or paying for treatment.

Rapid Cycling

Rapid cycling of bipolar symptoms is associated with more severe symptoms of the disorder. It refers to the experience of having a major depressive, manic, hypomanic, or mixed episode at least four times in the previous year, each cycle lasting for a relatively short time. The order of the moods or their combination does not matter. For a diagnosis of rapid cycling, the different moods must immediately follow one another, or a mood must be followed by a brief period free of extreme mood swings.

In extreme cases, some people rapid cycle several times a day. All told, 10 to 20 percent of bipolar patients experience rapid cycling, often in the first few years of the illness. It happens more often with bipolar II than bipolar I, but it can occur in both. It affects women, who account for 70 to 90 percent of the cases, much more often than men. It also tends to coincide with earlier onset; people who recycle have their first episode about four years earlier than people with nonrecycling bipolar disorder. This means they are more likely to be teenagers when they first show signs of the disorder.

CHAPTER 2

How Do You Know If You're Bipolar?

Mood changes are normal. They are part of what it means to be human. How can you tell if your ups and downs fall within a normal range or if they signal the presence of a problem that might require professional assistance? One sure indication of a problem would be if your fluctuating emotion made you so unhappy or dissatisfied that they seriously interfered with your life. The only way to determine for certain if you have bipolar disorder, however, is to consider your past and present medical and mental health history with the help of a specialist qualified to diagnose mental disorders. A doctor will look for specific criteria that point to the presence of bipolar disorder and eliminate other medical conditions that produce similar symptoms. The information in this chapter will give you a better idea of when you might benefit from treatment.

Mistaking Bipolar Disorder for "Normal"

Ironically, although we know more about bipolar disorder than we did just a few years ago, the fast pace of life and the stress people often feel today can make it difficult to tell if someone has bipolar disorder. Today, we do not just admire achievement; we admire over-the-top achievement. Hence, the hypomanic side of bipolar disorder might, for a time anyway, fit well with someone's career and lifestyle—unless and until it sabotages them.

People might marvel at how much an individual with bipolar disorder accomplishes, and wonder where all her energy comes from. Then, when her mood shifts to depression, people might attribute it to working too hard—which leads to the conclusion that all she needs is a little rest. Or people might wonder why this highly motivated person is so profoundly plagued with self-doubt.

In other situations, such an individual might suddenly turn on close associates or loved ones. People might dismiss this unsocial behavior with clichés: She has a larger-than-life personality or does not suffer fools gladly. Acquaintances might conclude that this irritable person, like others who are highly driven to succeed, is easier to admire from a safe distance.

Again, observations such as these are consistent with bipolar disorder, but they tell you little about your mental health. You need to see a doctor to know for sure.

Essential

It is neither accurate nor helpful to think of bipolar disorder as "romantic" or "appealing." When you hear someone comment, "He is probably bipolar, but for him it's a good thing, because it helps him accomplish so much," you can be sure the speaker lacks a fundamental understanding of the illness. As many people living with bipolar disorder know, it must be viewed as a serious condition requiring treatment because when it is out of control, it can destroy lives.

However successful a person with bipolar disorder might be for a time, treatment is still essential. The mania is still destined to get out of control, and a seemingly successful person might end up making tragically unfortunate choices. Also, the depressive part of the cycle will likely appear, and with it the possible threat of suicide. When someone who seems to be successful mysteriously commits suicide—or, short of that, suddenly engages in self-destructive behavior—it is possible she has bipolar disorder but does not know it.

A key indicator of your need for help will be your dissatisfaction and unhappiness. However, many people with bipolar disorder can't recognize that they are engaging in self-destructive behavior. In these cases, a clash with an authority, often the law, eventually brings them to a doctor's notice.

Is Your Culture a Culprit?

Some countries appear to have higher rates of bipolar disorder than others. Studies conducted in the 1980s and 1990s suggested that lifetime rates of bipolar I disorder across nations varied from 0.5 percent to 1.5 percent, with Asian countries enjoying the lowest rates.

 Fact

Mood disorders are common all over the world and take a significant toll in terms of health and productivity. In the mid-1990s, The World Health Organization estimated that bipolar depression was the sixth leading cause of disability worldwide.

The lifetime prevalence rates of all subtypes of bipolar disorders were estimated to be between 3 percent and 6.5 percent, but it is not clear why the rates vary. It could be due to differences in how the information was gathered, diagnostic practices, or genetics. Another possibility is differences in cultures. The only consistent risk factor found in these studies appeared to be marital status, with divorced or separated individuals more at risk. It's possible that stress and problems with interpersonal relationships, including lack of social support, could account for differences in the number of cases in different countries.

General Warning Signs

Although it is often extreme, bipolar behavior has some features in common with normal behavior. People who don't have bipolar disorder can, from time to time, exhibit similar characteristics, particularly under stress. Crisis situations, major life changes, and so-called recreational drug use can produce such behaviors. Therefore, the presence of certain thoughts and behaviors does not automatically mean you have bipolar disorder; there can be many other explanations. Still, it is useful to be aware of key bipolar warning signs.

- **Sudden changes in behavior.** These can include changes in eating and sleeping patterns, energy levels and confidence in personal or professional activities.
- **Poor concentration skills.** You rarely finish a project, or do much more than necessary to complete a project. You might stay up all night working on something, only to destroy it the next morning—as if to create and destroy were part of the same process.
- **Extreme arrogance.** You might talk about nothing but yourself, and always in the most superlative of terms. You always expect praise, even for feats of questionable value. You might make up facts about your past achievements, social connections, and family history.
- **Inappropriate anger.** If a situation would not evoke anger in most people but causes you to feel outrage, there is cause for concern. This is especially true if you hit and throw things or destroy property.
- **Excessive meddling.** If you are intent on telling other people what to do, cannot stop thinking about what they should do, and spend large amounts of time talking about other people, you should find out why you have become so obsessed.

- **Rapid cycling of moods.** If your moods shift drastically and frequently, you should investigate. This might mean your mood episodes last months before shifting or you could experience dramatic mood shifts in the span of a few hours.
- **Sexual compulsion.** It is not unusual for a person with bipolar disorder to make inappropriate sexual advances, take dangerous risks, destroy personal relationships, move in with strangers, or use up finances in order to have sex.
- **Imaginary aches and pains.** If you experience body aches and pains but multiple doctors find nothing wrong with you, it is a good idea to get professional help to examine your thoughts and behavior patterns.

 Alert

Bipolar disorder is expensive. The annual cost of treatment for one patient is around $19,000. Overall, health care bills for someone with bipolar disorder are four times that of someone who does not have the disorder. While treatment of bipolar disorder costs society plenty, not treating it costs even more; about $44 billion is due to lost wages and compensation, suicide, and lost productivity. It can also take a toll on family members who act or try to act as caregivers.

- **Mood changes with the seasons.** Some people with bipolar disorder become depressed in winter and manic or hypomanic in spring or summer. Others experience the reverse.
- **Inappropriate risk taking.** You might engage in dangerous relationships, financial ventures, dishonesty, crime, or physical activities to fulfill a self-destructive desire for excitement.
- **Psychosis.** The extreme detachment from reality that characterizes a psychotic episode can be caused by many things, ranging from drugs to metabolic diseases to several mental disorders, including bipolar disorder. Symptoms

often include delusions—false but firmly held beliefs—and/ or hallucinations, which involve hearing or seeing things that don't exist. For some people, a psychotic break from reality is the first sign of bipolar disorder.

What Puts You at Risk of Bipolar?

Bipolar disorder is not your fault; it is a brain disorder that is influenced by many factors including interactions between your biology and your environment. Scientists have identified some of the factors that are associated with the disorder. Unfortunately, we don't know how these factors interact to produce bipolar disorder. Familiarity with the risk factors can help you understand the condition and help your doctor reach an accurate diagnosis.

Risk Factors You Can't Control

No matter how well we care for ourselves, some things will always be beyond our control. While we can exercise, eat a healthy diet, get regular medical checkups, seek to reduce stress, and maintain strong social ties, factors such as genetics, age, gender, and unforeseen stressful events will always influence our health.

Your Genes

Bipolar disorder has a strong genetic component. In other words, it tends to run in families. Someone who has had a family member diagnosed with depression or bipolar disorder has an increased risk of developing the same or another brain disorder.

Even if you aren't sure if one of your family members or ancestors had a mental disorder, it is important to discuss, as completely as you can, your family history with your physician. A relative with a history of unstable behavior could be a significant factor for a psychiatrist who is trying to answer questions about your health.

Your Age and Gender

Age is a significant factor when estimating the chances you have bipolar disorder. Some people develop the illness when they are in their forties or fifties, but most begin to show signs of it when they are between the ages of fifteen and thirty years.

Another factor you have no control over is your sex. It won't affect your chances of having bipolar disorder, but it may affect how the symptoms affect you. Women are three times as likely as men to have rapid-cycling symptoms. This means they are more likely to have big mood shifts at least four times a year or, in some cases, more than one mood swing in a week, or even in a day.

Risk Factors You May Be Able to Influence

Just as some people can tolerate more pain than others, some people are able to tolerate stress better than others. While it often is not possible to avoid stressful situations, you might learn to limit your exposure to them and learn ways to better handle stress you can't avoid. Stressing yourself by abusing drugs and alcohol is another risk factor you can get help to control.

Stress

Stress is a response to psychological pressure and demands that others put on us or that we put on ourselves. Jobs, bosses and coworkers, school, teachers and fellow students, family, friends and strangers, money, and poor health are a few common sources of stress. Many scientists believe that stress can trigger bipolar episodes and may contribute to the onset of the disorder. Sleep disruption resulting from stress is one factor.

You may be able to link your first bipolar episode to some stress event in your life. This might have been the breakup of a relationship, giving birth, losing a job, or other major life change.

Some people with bipolar disorder endured a stressful event that was outside their control—childhood abuse, for example.

Professional counseling can help people deal with the scars left by past abuse. Other types of stress can be controlled to varying degrees.

While you often can't prevent a major life change, there are ways to cope with the effects of routine stress. Exercise and/or meditation, including yoga, help some people. Psychological counseling has also proven to be effective. In some cases, medications may be necessary.

Substance Abuse

Many people with bipolar disorder self-medicate with street drugs and/or alcohol. While the escape offered by substance abuse or addiction provides a distraction for a brief time, it can make the symptoms worse over the long term. You will find that alcohol and other street drugs increase your chances of having a manic or depressed episode and increase their duration. Addiction will make your chances of controlling bipolar disorder slim. If you have a substance abuse problem, you will probably need treatment if you want to get off the drugs or alcohol and control the symptoms of bipolar disorder.

Behavioral Extremes and Private Thoughts

Behavioral extremes, in combination with other factors such as your medical history, may be an indication of bipolar disorder. If you—or someone you know—exhibit extreme behavior that consistently troubles you or others, check with a qualified doctor. You may not have bipolar disorder, but there is no harm or shame in finding out. Whatever you discover will help by either reassuring you or leading you to treatment. Some more common examples of behavioral extremes include:

- **Busy bee/slug:** Person who is doing many things at once or is utterly listless and lethargic.
- **Chatterbox/silent type:** Person who either cannot stop talking or rarely speaks.

- **Life of the party/recluse:** Person who is either the charismatic center of attention or cannot wait to unplug the phone and stay away from everyone.
- **Optimist/pessimist:** Person who acts like he's either extraordinarily lucky or seems to find nothing good in life. In the optimistic phase, there is often a strong interest and belief in superstition or mystical predestiny. Then, in the downward swing to pessimism, life seems utterly meaningless and chaotic, fated to bring ruin.

While external behaviors are often signs of bipolar disorder, internal thoughts can also provide clues. Much like behaviors, the private thoughts of people with bipolar disorder also tend to gravitate toward the extremes.

- **"I am happy, confident, and loved."/"I am sad, frightened, and alone."** Person might be euphoric one moment, depressed the next. Such a person feels utterly at ease and secure or else anxious and frightened.
- **"I feel things too strongly."/"I never feel much of anything."** A person may feel that she is the only person in the room (or in the family or on the face of the earth) who has deep, honest emotional responses, or she believes she is the least emotional person.
- **"I am better than other people."/"I am worse than other people."** Some people feel bored by everyone and vastly superior or feel utterly unworthy of anyone's companionship. Often, these people seem most eager to make friends at first, but then become extremely critical or short-tempered.
- **"I love life."/"I hate life."** Some people feel as if life could not be better, or think that everything is useless, meaningless, foolish, ugly, or grotesque. At either extreme, a person might begin to hear voices or experience hallucinations. At the depressive extreme, the person thinks of suicide.

If you are concerned that someone you know might have bipolar disorder, you can encourage her to see a doctor, or at least read up on the topic. More information will be provided later on how you might try to do this as tactfully as possible. Of course, identifying the symptoms of bipolar disorder can be tricky. People may be more likely to recognize the symptoms after being treated—medication makes the contrast between symptomatic and nonsymptomatic behavior much clearer. The sad irony is that many untreated patients are more likely to believe nothing is wrong with them, or that nothing can be done to help.

See a Doctor

If there is a possibility that you or someone you care about has bipolar disorder, the only way to be certain is to see a doctor. You can start by visiting your general practitioner (GP). Even if your GP decides you have bipolar disorder and prescribes medication, you should always get a second opinion from a psychiatrist. A general practitioner is good for diagnosing more common ailments, but he should refer you to a psychiatrist if there is a possibility you have a serious mental condition.

 Alert

Psychologists may have PhDs or master's degrees. Psychiatrists are medical doctors and have MDs or DOs (Doctor of Osteopathy). Many maladies are helped through psychology, but if your problem is bipolar disorder, only a medical doctor can diagnose it and prescribe medication. Psychologists can help you by providing therapy, which can greatly improve the quality of your life after you have been diagnosed. The goal is to get you to think and feel differently about yourself so you can live your daily life in more productive ways and avoid relapses.

Do not confuse a psychologist with a psychiatrist. Psychologists address mental and emotional problems from the standpoint of life experience, but they cannot practice medicine. Bipolar disorder requires medical treatment.

Diagnosis

To some extent, doctors are at the mercy of patients when making a diagnosis; they can only speculate if you don't tell them everything that is relevant. So, do not be afraid, and do not be ashamed—answer every question fully and honestly. Perhaps some day there will be a clinical test that will indicate when someone has bipolar disorder. In the meantime, honest self-reports provided to your medical doctor are the only way to get an accurate diagnosis. Your doctor will ask you to describe your energy, thoughts, and behavioral patterns as well as asking you a series of specific questions. He also might ask you to take one or more standardized tests to help him reach the correct diagnosis. While it can be frustrating to have to try different treatments or recheck symptoms, try to look at the inconvenience as evidence that a good psychiatrist is never casual in diagnosing people with a serious mental disorder.

Essential

Bipolar disorder diagnosis requires patience on the part of both the patient and doctor. At present, only about 20 percent of patients receive a full diagnosis in a year or less. For most people struggling with this condition, it takes at least 10 years between the onset of symptoms and a correct diagnosis.

Be a Good Patient

As a patient, there are two personas you should avoid. First, don't be the eager-to-please patient who tries to second guess what the doctor wants to hear in order to provide it. For example, when asked by the doctor how things are going, a patient might respond with the knee-jerk response, "Fine." This patient so wants the doctor to be right that even if some aspects of the treatment are not working, she does not admit it. If a doctor indicates he is predicting a certain response from a treatment, the patient might report confirmation of it even if it isn't working.

On the other hand, the rebellious patient might insist that nothing is going well even if it is. A patient often rebels against treatment when he feels he is being forced to see a doctor or does not really want to get better. The rebellious patient will scrupulously avoid mentioning certain things or talk about them in a way that makes them seem more or less important than they are. The overriding theme will be that the treatment is not working; which is to say the doctor does not know how to connect with him and/or that no one in the world can.

A responsible psychiatrist will not make a diagnosis of bipolar disorder (or anything else) simply for the sake of making a diagnosis. It is hoped that once given medication, you will notice an improvement after a period of testing and adjustment. However, if you feel no different—or feel worse—you need to be honest with your doctor and tell her what works and what doesn't. Diagnosis is a collaborative process between doctor and patient. Your mental health is at stake; it won't benefit you if you are passive about it or sabotage your doctor's effort to diagnose and help you.

Get a Second Opinion

Being treated for bipolar disorder is a lifetime proposition, so you owe it to yourself to seek out a second opinion. This is especially important if the medication you are taking does not seem to be working. The same holds true in reverse. If your first doctor says you do not have bipolar disorder but you still think you might have it, see what a second doctor has to say.

Beware of Misdiagnosis

The most common errors in the misdiagnosis of bipolar disorder are confusing one type of bipolar disorder for another and checking only for depression. If you are being tested for depression by a psychiatrist, you should ask if the doctor is also considering the possibility of mania. If you are diagnosed with a form of bipolar disorder, you should ask which type it is. Again, it also is in your best interest to seek a second opinion.

If you start a regimen of treatment, you should find out all you can about the medication you are taking. A good doctor will answer all of your questions, but you can also use resources such as the Internet to find out even more. Just be sure you use reliable sources such as those provided by major hospitals and authorities like the Mayo Clinic, the National Institute of Mental Health, etc. Once on medication, you need to be scrupulously honest with your doctor and yourself about what is or is not changing in your moods and physical condition.

Fact

According to the Depression and Bipolar Support Alliance, 87 percent of patients report being satisfied with the care they receive from their doctors. Thus, despite the fact that diagnosis can be a drawn-out process, patients seem to be generally pleased with how they are treated, both in terms of their illnesses and as human beings.

Don't Let Limitations Stop You

No matter how delicate your financial situation is, it's worthwhile to get a first and second opinion, a sound diagnosis, and, if necessary, treatment. If you live in a relatively small community and do not have access to a variety of psychiatrists, then see one in the next town over or in the nearest big city. Your mental well-being is more important than inconvenience or money if you can afford it.

What if the second psychiatrist's diagnosis is different than the first? In this case, you might want to consider how the two doctors came to their conclusions. Ask as many questions as possible of both doctors. You can also compare the two doctors in terms of their years of experience, references from other patients, and how well each seems to understand you and is willing to listen to you. If you're still in doubt, seek out a third opinion if possible.

Once you have found a medication or a combination of medications that work for you, stay on it! No matter how stable your moods have become, you will need to keep taking your medication(s). Your moods are stable because of medication, so if you stop taking it, the extreme mood swings are likely to return.

Evolving Knowledge of Bipolar Disorder

People with bipolar disorder can consider themselves relatively fortunate to be diagnosed in today's world, when so much more is known about influences, symptoms, and treatments for mental disorders compared to much of the last century.

Important Trends

In the 1950s, the era of pharmacological treatment for mental illness began and rapidly decreased the number of people confined to psychiatric hospitals. Medications would see many refinements over the ensuing decades, but the finding that bipolar disorder could be treated by the right combination of medications radically altered the medical community's ability to clear out mental hospitals and improve people's lives.

In 1949, Australian psychiatrist John Cade published results demonstrating the antimanic effects of lithium. By 1970, the usefulness of this simple element had been established.

The hunt for genes that might contribute to bipolar and other disorders continues. In parallel with this hunt, scientists continue to confirm the factual basis of many long-assumed features of the disorder. They've established, for example, that most of those with bipolar disorder also have been hospitalized, suffer from other illnesses such as alcohol or substance abuse, and have missed work.

Why Is There No Cure?

Medical science has already cured many diseases; now it is faced with complex diseases with multiple causes, often multiple genetic influences, and complicated interactions between the environment and genetics.

L. Essential

One of the most outspoken advocates for education on bipolar disorder is actress Patty Duke. In her autobiography, *Call Me Anna*, she writes frankly about the extreme mood swings that hampered her life until she was diagnosed. She provides the reader with an accurate picture of what it is like to live with untreated bipolar disorder.

The physical brain produces feelings, emotions, and a sense of self. While neuroscience has made significant advances in recent decades, it has a very long way to go before it can provide enough understanding about how the brain works to provide cures to complex mental disorders.

Another reason progress has been slow is cost. It takes money, lots of money, to advance basic scientific understanding. Many health care advocates and researchers feel not enough money is devoted to this type of research.

For instance, many genes have been linked in some way to different mental illnesses. We know that brain function depends on communication between its different parts. These neural circuits are almost certainly abnormal in mental illness. Combining knowledge about a patient's unique set of genes with an improved understanding of how different genes affect the brain's neural circuitry could lead to new insights and ultimately better treatments for a variety of mental disorders, including bipolar disorder.

With money and effort, future progress may someday result in researchers being able to predict which treatments will work best for which patient. Beyond that, in years to come, researchers hope to see ways to predict and prevent the onset of the illness.

CHAPTER 3

Comparing Bipolar Disorder to Other Disorders

The presence of fairly strong mood swings does not necessarily indicate bipolar disorder. Several other disorders can produce similar symptoms, a fact that can and does lead to misdiagnoses. To receive the best treatment, it's essential to determine if symptoms are caused by bipolar disorder or by another condition.

Varieties of Personality and Mood Disorders

If you suspect you have bipolar disorder, you might want to learn about other mood disorders to compare symptoms. It is possible you do not have a mental disorder. You may be under extraordinary stress, and could benefit from professional advice to help deal with it. Another possibility is you have a mood, personality, or anxiety disorder, but not bipolar disorder. A third possibility is that you do have bipolar disorder, in which case you should begin treatment at once. Finally, there is the possibility that you have features of more than one disorder, a mixed diagnosis. It is important to consider this possibility because the presence of other disorders can complicate treatment in several ways.

First, stresses and symptoms associated with other disorders can exacerbate bipolar symptoms by triggering manic or depressive episodes. Second, the presence of other disorders can make it harder to treat bipolar disorder. For example, if another mood disorder also requires medication, it might not be compatible with treatments for bipolar disorder. Finally, other mood, anxiety, and personality disorders can make it quite difficult to detect bipolar disorder.

Borderline Personality Disorder (BPD)

The label "borderline" reflects the belief held in the past that this disorder was a borderline psychosis. Today, it's recognized as a disorder of a person's core personality, with persistent traits.

Unstable Moods

Borderline personality (BPD) is associated with strong, sometimes shifting feelings and behaviors, which in turn contribute to an insecure personal and professional life. Someone might impulsively quit a job, end a relationship, or make an enemy out of a friend due to real or imagined fears of abandonment, disappointment, or perceived threats.

Essential

People with BPD may have difficulty coping with boredom. They cannot last long at a repetitive job, and on a personal level can equate boredom with cruelty—as though someone were intentionally plotting to hurt their feelings by not engaging their attention.

This insecurity and instability can result in aggressive impulses, which can be expressed as anger toward others, injury to self, substance abuse, binge eating or spending, or high-risk sex. Much of the anger is self-directed, and can involve self-injury or suicide attempts.

Poor Social Skills

Some dominant traits of BPD are fear of abandonment, extreme sensitivity to rejection, and frustration at being misunderstood. Consequently, relationships tend to be unstable and riddled with conflict.

A person with this personality disorder has trouble with honest self-reflection. She doesn't have a realistic sense of personal strengths and weaknesses, and will blame others rather than herself for contributing to unpleasant situations and confrontations.

Connection to Bipolar Disorder

Not only can someone with bipolar disorder have a borderline personality, BPD symptoms can sometimes be misconstrued as indications of bipolar disorder. This is because they include features similar to mania: sudden changes in mood swings, impulsiveness, irritability, wasteful spending, risky sex, and extreme impatience and suicidal thoughts.

It's easy to appreciate how someone whose moods change quickly due to rapid-cycling bipolar symptoms can be confused with someone with BPD. One key difference is bipolar disorder is an episodic mood disorder, with extreme moods that come and go. A person with BPD always shows traits of that personality. Also, someone with a personality disorder won't have full-blown mania or hypomania.

 Fact

Behavior therapy is one method for treating borderline personality disorder. One goal is to get patients to view the things they say and do—and the things that subsequently happen to them—in less extreme terms. Antidepressants and mood stabilizers are sometimes used in concert with individual and group therapy.

A person with both bipolar disorder and a borderline personality might be more vulnerable to making unwise, impetuous decisions. For example, a rude nurse could be perceived as a valid excuse for an individual with both disorders to discontinue medication, despite the fact that it could be a disastrous decision.

Attention Deficit
Hyperactivity Disorder (ADHD)

Attention Deficit Hyperactivity Disorder (ADHD) has been well studied in children who have short attention spans, difficulty sitting still, and problems concentrating—handicaps that often result in disciplinary problems and poor academic performance. It is often treated with a stimulant called Ritalin, which has a calming effect on such children. Distinguishing ADHD and bipolar disorder in children can be a difficult challenge. ADHD in adults has received less attention.

Essential

Adults with ADHD are sometimes prescribed medication. They also may be encouraged to pick careers that involve a minimum of repetition. Exercising during breaks can work off excess energy. There are also ways to compensate for a limited ability to concentrate for extended lengths of time. For example, if concentration might wander during lectures or meetings, a tape recorder can capture important points to be studied later.

Less Obvious with Maturity

Symptoms of ADHD, particularly the urge to move, tend to fade in most people as they reach late adolescence and adulthood. A few, however, retain all the symptoms of the disorder, while others retain enough to interfere with their ability to function. Thus, it is often less obvious that an adult is experiencing ADHD.

Connection to Bipolar Disorder

The symptoms of adults with ADHD might resemble some of the manic or hypomanic episodes of bipolar disorder. Besides an inability to concentrate, they may include tendencies to impatiently interrupt others, mismanage money, and make impetuous changes and decisions. Also, occasional frustration from failing to get organized or finish things might at times seem like a brief lapse into depression and despair.

Bipolar symptoms may be more severe if ADHD is present. If they are not both present, they may be distinguished by the consistency of ADHD symptoms and the come-and-go mood swings common to bipolar disorder.

Post-Traumatic Stress and Other Anxiety Disorders

It is not unusual—estimates range from 60 to 90 percent—for people with bipolar disorder to have an anxiety disorder at the same time. Anxiety disorders include generalized anxiety, panic disorders, social phobias, and post-traumatic stress disorder (PTSD). Some symptoms of severe anxiety—agitation, restlessness, racing thoughts—can look like mania.

Dealing with Trauma

PTSD can result from traumatizing events: rape, torture, serious injury, kidnapping, abduction, acts of war, witnessing murder or other crimes, or getting caught in a natural disaster.

People with PTSD will avoid anything that raises stressful and painful memories. Anniversaries of the past event can be especially traumatic. Sometimes the trigger is more obvious, for example, the sound of a gunshot or a violent scene in a movie.

When a painful memory surfaces, symptoms include flashbacks, during which the trauma is relived, often with sounds and visions. Anxiety and depression are also common.

People with PTSD are often too frightened, embarrassed, or unable to explain what is happening to them. Even when loved ones know what they went through, traumatized people might think they are being a burden by discussing their problems. As a result, social relationships often become strained. Not surprisingly, people often turn to substance abuse to counter these feelings; addiction is common with PTSD.

Connection to Bipolar Disorder

One feature that can differentiate anxiety disorder from bipolar disorder is the link between the severity of symptoms and the degree of anxiety: the greater the anxiety, the worse the symptoms. Again, bipolar symptoms are more episodic in nature.

 Fact

People from all walks of life can experience PTSD. War veterans, of course, are frequent victims. Veterans of the Vietnam War are around fifty times more likely than other U.S. men to be homeless, suffer from mood disorders, be unable to work, and have attempted suicide. As might be predicted, the most recent U.S. wars in Iraq and Afghanistan are producing another wave of men and women with PTSD.

It is very important that you tell your psychiatrist about any worries, fears, or anxieties you have and about any tragic or traumatic events you have experienced. Your doctor needs to know this information so he can determine if you have both an anxiety disorder and bipolar disorder. Only when an accurate diagnosis is made can the best treatment plan be devised.

Intermittent Explosive Disorder (IED)

Outbursts of intermittent explosive disorder (IED) are intense and sudden attacks of anger and rage that go beyond a normal response to a slight provocation or stressful situation. The person with IED is not always full of rage, and sometimes responds with an appropriate degree of displeasure. But she is also prone to violent outbursts in which she loses control of her aggressive impulses. This can result in serious damage to others or to property.

IED episodes begin and end abruptly. They can last for minutes or hours. Commonly, people break objects or destroy property, but they can also injure themselves or others. During an episode of IED, an individual often feels confused, as though confusion were fueling the rage. Sometimes, the person reports having no memory of the outburst.

Alert

A common manifestation of IED is road rage. Some drivers with IED might respond irrationally to real or perceived instances of irresponsible or inconsiderate driving by others. Sometimes the resulting confrontations result in serious injury or death. The behavior of the other driver acts as a catalyst for anger over some deeper issue. Males in their thirties are the likeliest perpetrators of road rage.

Diagnosing IED

IED is classified as an impulse-control disorder. The diagnosis is made when it is apparent that a person is free of symptoms associated with other mental disorders. It also must be apparent that the violent episodes are not linked to alcohol or drug abuse. In other words, a person with IED might seem mentally healthy if he did not have uncontrollable outbursts.

Once diagnosed, IED might be treated with medication, therapy, or both. There is some evidence to suggest it is neurological in nature, since some people with it have abnormal brain wave (EEG) patterns.

Connection to Bipolar Disorder

Some evidence suggests there may be an association between IED and substance abuse, anxiety, eating, and mood disorders, including bipolar disorder.

People in a manic or depressive phase of bipolar disorder can display sudden rages for no apparent reason. If delusional or hallucinating, they might be confused, and afterward remember only some of their actions. Remorse experienced after an IED episode might be confused with depression. Thus, it is important that a thorough evaluation be made to distinguish the pattern of rages and their relationship in time to episodes of mania, depression, and relative calm.

Schizophrenia and Schizoaffective Disorder

Unlike bipolar disorder, schizophrenia and schizoaffective disorder are classified as psychotic disorders, not mood disorders. Nevertheless, their symptoms overlap enough to make it sometimes difficult—particularly when a doctor is first getting to know a patient—to determine exactly which disorders are present.

Defining Features

Schizophrenia is a severe brain disease that causes a person to lose touch with reality, often due to the effects of psychotic symptoms including delusions, hallucinations, disorganized speech, and bizarre, disorganized behavior. Other serious symptoms include impaired intellectual ability, blunted emotions, lack of motivation, and an inability to experience pleasure. It is often, but not always, a chronic condition. Mood stabilizers, so helpful for treating bipolar disorder, do not relieve symptoms of schizophrenia.

Schizoaffective disorder is essentially a hybrid category with elements of psychotic and mood disorders. Patients with schizoaffective disorder have two or more of the schizophrenia symptoms described above as well as a major depressive, manic, or mixed episodes, all occurring in one uninterrupted period of time. If the episode is depressive, they are diagnosed with schizoaffective disorder, depressive type. If the episode includes a manic or mixed episode, or a manic or mixed plus a depressive episode, they are diagnosed with schizoaffective disorder, bipolar type.

Unlike schizophrenia, mood stabilizers can help people with schizoaffective bipolar disorder. In fact, some doctors regard it as a variant of bipolar I.

Connection to Bipolar Disorder

In schizophrenia, psychotic symptoms can be ongoing. In cases of bipolar disorder, psychotic symptoms are never present in the absence of a mood episode. It isn't easy to tell the difference between a bipolar mixed episode and a schizophrenic psychotic episode in a patient whose mental health history is unknown. The only way to tell is to wait and watch. When the mood episode subsides, psychotic symptoms will fade in bipolar disorder, but they will persist in schizophrenia.

Patients with schizoaffective disorder can present a more complicated challenge because they may have both manic and depressive episodes as well as psychosis. Again, observation can lead to a correct diagnosis because the psychotic symptoms will end when the mood episode ends in cases of bipolar disorder, but not with schizoaffective disorder.

Major Depressive Disorder and Substance Use Disorders

Some disorders are so closely associated with bipolar disorder that at times they seem to be inseparable. However, this is a superficial impression. Health risks like major depressive disorder (MDD) and substance use disorders are distinct problems with symptoms that may look like bipolar disorder at times, but should not be confused with it.

Major Depressive Disorder

MDD has the same symptoms seen in bipolar depressive episodes. The defining difference between the two mood disorders lies in the absence of past manic, hypomanic, or mixed episodes in MDD. Without a clinical test, the only way to tell the difference is to determine whether there is a history of such episodes. This is extremely difficult when the first sign of bipolar disorder is a depressive episode, something that happens in more than half the cases. Obviously, it is necessary to closely follow someone to see if they eventually experience mania in order to distinguish these two major mood disorders.

 Fact

Recreational drug use and abuse often results in symptoms similar to those of bipolar disorder. Recreational drugs fall into three main categories: stimulants, including powder cocaine, crack cocaine, and amphetamines; depressants, such as alcohol, tranquilizers, and barbiturates; and hallucinogens, which can be considered minor, like marijuana, or major, like LSD.

Substance Use Disorders

Many people with bipolar disorder—between 40 percent and 60 percent by some estimates—have a long-term substance use disorder as well. Usually, the drug of choice is alcohol, a depressant, but stimulants such as cocaine and amphetamines are also abused. Besides the health risks that come with substance abuse, alcohol and illegal substances can produce symptoms very similar to those of bipolar disorder, including depression and mixed and manic states. If someone's extreme moods end when the substance use ends, it suggests that the drugs and not bipolar disorder might be the cause. But it isn't easy to tell if someone who has stopped drinking, for example, is depressed because they gave up alcohol—a common reaction—or if they are experiencing a bipolar depressive episode. Stimulants mimic manic states by promoting risky and impulsive behaviors, reducing the need for sleep, and increasing the need for social and other stimulation.

The flip side of the association between bipolar disorder and substance use disorders is the tendency of mania to reduce limits of self-control, which frequently leads to use of illegal drugs. This can make it very difficult to determine quickly if someone has substance use disorder, major depressive disorder, bipolar disorder, or a combination.

CHAPTER 4

Who Gets Bipolar Disorder?

There doesn't appear to be one, stand-alone reason that explains why one person has a mood disorder and another does not. It's much more likely that several factors come together to increase the risk. Although gender, race, and income don't have much influence on risk, several other factors do. The most important is family history, with quite a bit of help, it seems, from some influences that originate outside a person's DNA. There is a popular belief that creative people are prone to bipolar disorder, and it is true that many accomplished people, past and present, have been linked to the disorder. Preliminary evidence supports this widely held view, although the studies are small in scale.

Important Factors

No one knows exactly how many people in the U.S. have bipolar disorder, since many are never diagnosed. But if the estimate of the National Institute of Mental Health is correct and the number approaches 6 million, it has a significant impact on life in the U.S. Understanding its risk factors is important for developing better ways to diagnose and treat it.

Age and Gender

Being over age fifteen but under thirty puts people in a high-risk category. Most cases appear in the early twenties and last twenty years or more. This means bipolar disorder tends to appear sooner than major depressive disorder. That is one reason why it is important to follow a young person closely for signs of bipolar disorder; otherwise, she could be misdiagnosed and receive inappropriate and even harmful treatment if bipolar is confused with MDD.

Men and women are equally susceptible. However, women differ from men in an important way: they are three times more likely to cycle rapidly through moods, a more serious form of the disorder.

 Fact

Although the Amish are no more likely than anyone else to have bipolar disorder, they often have more detailed records of their lineage, extending back hundreds of years. This is why researchers have studied the mood disorder in this group of people. The closeness of the community and the extensive documented histories makes it easier to study genetic factors influencing bipolar disorder, and to track symptoms in children.

Ethnicity, Geography, and Socioeconomic Status

There aren't huge differences in the rates of bipolar disorder around the world or among different racial groups. Those that have been noted might be explained by a tendency of doctors in some parts of the world to diagnose bipolar disorder as another disorder such as schizophrenia. A 2007 survey of 9,000 randomly sampled people representing the population of the U.S. turned up no differences based on ethnic background, race, or family income level.

Are Some People More Likely to Have Bipolar Disorder?

The evidence that bipolar disorder has a strong genetic component is overwhelming. It confirms that, indeed, some people are at a higher risk of developing it than others. But inheriting genes linked to the disorder still does not guarantee you will have bipolar symptoms. Other factors that increase the risk are:

- Being between ages fifteen and thirty
- Having blood relatives with the disorder
- Experiencing extremely stressful situations such as divorce or death of a loved one
- Abusing drugs or alcohol
  Source: The Mayo Clinic

No one knows how these factors interact with genes to cause bipolar disorder. And it is possible there are multiple pathways that can end with someone having severe mood fluctuations. What is certain is that sorting them out will not be easy.

Genes

Parents and siblings of someone with bipolar disorder are more likely to have the same disorder than someone with no family history. Even people who have an affected relative from a previous generation are more likely to be affected by it. In fact, of all the risk factors, family history is the strongest.

It's easier to know if someone in the immediate family showed signs of a mood disorder; many people can only guess if more distant relatives were ill in this way. Did a high-strung great uncle who sometimes turned violent have an undiagnosed mood disorder? Since many people lack detailed knowledge about the medical history of such ancestors, it is not unusual for them to be unsure if they are predisposed to bipolar or another mental disorder with a genetic basis.

Environmental Factors

Although they are powerful factors, genes alone do not completely determine a person's fate. Genes can be influenced by factors that originate outside the body.

An example of such an outside influence may be diet, a key part of a healthy lifestyle. Consuming omega-3 fatty acid, for example, is associated with several benefits, including cardiovascular health. Some studies indicate that consumption of seafood, which is rich in omega-3 fatty acid, lowers the risk of bipolar disorder. This doesn't mean that eating fish, other foods rich in the nutrient, or taking supplements will cure the disorder, but it does suggest that environmental factors can influence its prevalence.

Essential

While looking for differences in bipolar disorder rates in different countries, researchers found only one consistent risk factor: marital status, specifically separation and divorce. It's not clear if the stress of a broken marriage contributes to the development of the disorder or if bipolar symptoms place unbearable stress on a marriage.

Outside events that cause stress also increase risk. Problems giving birth and pregnancy itself may play a role. So, too, might birth date; being born in winter or spring comes with an increased risk. Perhaps mothers of infants born in these seasons were exposed to viruses that affected their offsprings' brains.

Famous People with Bipolar Disorder

A wide variety of well-known people have been linked to bipolar disorder. Long lists have been compiled to show that mental illness does not have to stop anyone from achieving success in life. It's not always easy, however, to know for sure if someone's name should be on the list.

The Price of Success?

Among entertainers who have been associated with the mood disorder are Stephen Frey, Spike Milligan, Richard Dreyfuss, Patty Duke, Carrie Fisher, Linda Hamilton, Margot Kidder, Vivien Leigh, Maurice Bernard, and Ben Stiller. Film directors said to be bipolar include Tim Burton and Joshua Logan.

Singers Rosemary Clooney, Connie Francis, and Charley Pride appear on the lists, too. Still other well-known personalities who have been linked to this illness are astronaut Buzz Aldrin, humorist Art Buchwald, television personality Dick Cavett, left-wing activist Abbie Hoffman, musician-raconteur Oscar Levant, Congressman Patrick J. Kennedy, and news host Jane Pauley.

 Fact

> The guessing game of bipolar versus other disorders is reflected in two legends: Marilyn Monroe and Judy Garland. Biographies on these famous stars make note of eating and sleeping problems as well as dramatic mood swings. Yet both stars also abused alcohol and other drugs. Was the drug use connected to bipolar disorder or did they just abuse drugs?

Some of the above celebrities have published memoirs describing their experiences with bipolar disorder. Others have discussed their medical history with the press.

Past Accomplishments

Many others not listed above are rumored to have the mood disorder. The same is true of many famous people of the past. The list of past musicians, artists, writers, and statesmen fill pages and includes names like Vincent Van Gogh, Robert Schumann, and Emily Dickinson. It's important to remember, however, that many mood, personality, and anxiety disorders as well as other medical conditions can produce symptoms like those seen in bipolar disorder. When combined with the lack of detailed medical records, it's difficult to be certain that any particular individual had bipolar disorder. However, since the disorder is so prevalent, it is likely that many famous, creative people in the past had some form of the disease.

 Question

What political leaders had bipolar disorder?
The behavior of statesmen has been studied for evidence of unipolar or bipolar symptoms. Abraham Lincoln, Theodore Roosevelt, and Winston Churchill are among the colorful and influential historical figures that experienced extreme, at times debilitating, moods.

The list of artists, writers, and musicians who apparently struggled with at least some form of depression or showed signs of bipolar tendencies is long and impressive. It should convince people that the apparent presence of depressive or bipolar symptoms need not prevent someone from achieving extraordinary success in life. However, remember that not everyone with bipolar disorder can be expected to have exceptional talents. Civilization is based on the efforts and support of people who live decent, moderately productive lives. If you can achieve that, you are accomplishing a great deal.

Bipolar Creativity

More than other mental illnesses, mood disorders have been linked to some degree of success and accomplishment. For centuries, people have suggested that talent or genius is somehow linked to what used to be called madness. The observation that some gifted people seem more sensitive or high-strung supports the suspicion that there is a link between mental instability and genius. (Of course, a prima-donna nature could also be due to insecurity, which by itself could account for extraordinary ambition and effort to succeed as a way to compensate.)

Genes Again

For rare individuals, some features of mania may contribute to periods of intense creative efforts that result in impressive accomplishments. It is possible that the genes that predispose someone to bipolar disorder are closely linked to genes that influence creativity. This might explain the results of one study that found relatives of people with bipolar disorder are more likely to be successful, or at least successful in the sense of earning more money. It is also possible that many creative people have features of bipolar disorder without having the more serious symptoms; they might lie on a different part of the bipolar spectrum that some psychiatrists believe exists.

 Fact

Comedian Spike Milligan became famous as the writer and star of the British radio program "The Goon Show," on which he performed with another famous comedian, Peter Sellers. Milligan, who had bipolar disorder, told an interviewer, "Van Gogh was a manic-depressive. He had to paint. I had to write. I really mean 'had to,' like it was easing, like it was lubricating my way out of this terrible blackness." Source: The documentary *The Life and Legacy of Spike Milligan*

Evidence of a Link

When thirty writers attending the Iowa Writer's Workshop were surveyed, thirteen of them (43 percent) reported having some type of bipolar disorder. Four (13 percent) had bipolar I, and nine (30 percent) had bipolar II. If unipolar depression was included, twenty-four of the thirty (80 percent) reported being affected by a mood disorder. Alcohol abuse was also common among this group.

A study of forty-seven writers in the United Kingdom found that over 6 percent had been treated for bipolar disorder and more than 38 percent had been treated for some type of mood disorder.

A survey of fifteen abstract expressionist artists in the 1950s found that about half had experienced mental illness, mostly mood disorders. Again, alcohol abuse was prevalent among them.

The result of each of these surveys is consistent with a link between mood disorders and creativity, but they are small samples. It will take larger and more exhaustive studies to definitively prove it, but these preliminary findings are intriguing. It is safe to say at this time that there is likely a relationship between creativity and bipolar disorder, and perhaps creativity and the presence of other bipolar and mental disorders in relatives.

Reality Check

Most people by definition are not extraordinarily gifted, talented, or creative. The same is true of most people with mood disorders. Mania can have superficially positive effects at first: more energy, ideas, and social confidence. But over time, mania gets out of control in most cases, making it impossible to use these changes in a productive way. Instead, they devolve into destructive behaviors like unsafe sex, indiscriminate spending, reckless actions, deep depressions, and suicidal thoughts.

Does Treatment Destroy Creativity?

While some people worry that taking medicines will turn them into "zombies" or "vegetables," those who make their living being creative generally report this is not true. In fact, the overwhelming majority of the writers surveyed in the first two studies summarized above received welcome treatment for their disorders. And a review of lithium use among artists in 1970 revealed that more then three-quarters of them claimed the bipolar disorder treatment did not affect, or else improved, their creativity.

This counters the claim that treatments such as lithium inevitably result in diminished sensations, what has been described as a "flattening out" effect. There are side effects, but many creative people have testified that they are more productive with than without treatment.

 Question

Does lithium have any other positive effects besides controlling bipolar mood changes?
It may reduce dementia. That is the conclusion of a 2010 Danish study, which found that people who took lithium had lower rates of dementia than people who took antipsychotics, antidepressants, or anticonvulsants.

If doses are kept as low as possible, and supplemental and substituted medications are used when necessary, there is an excellent chance that treatment will improve rather than dampen your creative potential.

Women and Bipolar Disorder

In addition to their own health, some women struggling with a mood disorder have an additional worry: the health of their unborn children. A mother's mental and physical health can affect her children as well as herself.

Pregnancy

If a woman with bipolar disorder becomes pregnant or is thinking about it, she should discuss it with her psychiatrist, obstetrician/gynecologist, and family doctor. Obviously, the potential effects on a fetus of any medication taken during pregnancy must be considered carefully. This is certainly true of medications used to treat bipolar disorder.

Don't stop taking your medications suddenly if you realize you are pregnant or have decided to become pregnant. This could result in serious mood episodes that could jeopardize your health and the health of your unborn child. But do get professional advice as soon as possible about how you should manage a mood disorder and a pregnancy at the same time.

 Alert

Some bipolar disorder medications can affect pregnancy. Some cause birth defects, so it is important to discuss the issue with your doctor. If you don't want to get pregnant, ask your doctor about birth control methods that would be best for you, since some bipolar disorder medications can interfere with their effectiveness. If you want to become pregnant, talk to your doctor to work out an appropriate treatment plan.

You might find you can change medications, continue with the ones you are taking, or slowly cut back on them, depending on your doctor's advice. You and your doctor will have to balance the risks posed by medications with the risk of recurring mood episodes.

The good news is pregnancy itself does not appear to increase the risk of having a bipolar episode.

After Pregnancy

The same isn't true following birth, when the odds are in favor of a recurrence of symptoms including postpartum depression or psychosis. Perhaps it is stress induced by hormonal changes or lack of sleep, but it is, unfortunately, common in women with bipolar disorder. You owe it to yourself, your newborn, and your family to consider this possibility very carefully. If it happens, immediate treatment is essential.

There are some steps you can take to protect yourself and your child:

- Get to your doctor at the first sign of postpartum illness, depression, mania, or psychosis. Don't stop or change your medications except under medical supervision.
- Arrange to have regular, frequent doctor visits or contacts for the first six to eight months after giving birth.
- Get help caring for your infant. Seek out and take advantage of any offer of assistance from a responsible, qualified relative, friend, or social services employee. Use the time away to rest and do something just for yourself.

Bipolar Disorder in Perspective

Genetics now provides the best clue we have for answering the question why some people and not others develop mood disorders. It appears that some people are born with genetic variations, which under the influence of certain environmental factors produce specific, still poorly understood changes in the brain that result in wild mood swings.

Playing with the Genes You Are Dealt

Having bipolar disorder appears to be the result of having biological bad luck, something completely out of your control. It may help a little to keep in mind that nearly everyone develops maladies, ailments, and serious problems over a lifetime. Living with bipolar disorder is not easy, and it is frequently difficult. Yet the same could be said for many other serious mental or physical ailments. If you have bipolar disorder, treat it with the utmost seriousness because you need to protect yourself from its effects. At the same time, try to remember that many other people have different and sometimes just as challenging burdens. And some struggle with even greater burdens.

Since mood disorders are now treatable in most cases, it might be useful to recall that many other ailments are not yet treatable at all. If you respond well to treatment, as most people do, consider yourself fortunate. Although you will be seriously challenged, by comparison with many worst-case scenarios, you are nevertheless fortunate because effective treatments are available.

A Bipolar Bottom Line

Bipolar disorder can be a long-term, sometimes chronic condition that can incapacitate you if left untreated. It can disrupt not only your life, but the lives of those close to you. Fortunately, medications and psychological counseling are available that help the overwhelming majority of people. Although symptoms may linger and periodically return for as many as half of those whose treatment successfully reduces the number and intensity of their mood swings, it is possible to live a happy and productive life after being diagnosed with this mood disorder.

CHAPTER 5

What Causes Bipolar Disorder?

As scientists learn more about bipolar disorder, it becomes clearer that multiple factors appear to cause and increase the risk of having this illness.

Biological Differences

Sophisticated imaging equipment allows scientists to take pictures of the living brain and record its activity without harming volunteers. Medical researchers can observe living brains using advanced imaging devices, super sophisticated cameras of sorts, to take neuroimages.

The Brain Looks Different

The CT (computerized tomography) scan takes thousands of thin x-ray pictures from different angles and then uses computer software to create a 3D image of the brain. MRI (magnetic resonance imaging) records the magnetic properties of atoms in the brain after they have been exposed to electromagnetic waves. Again, computer software transforms the information into a revealing picture.

Structural brain imaging reveals differences in several parts of the brain in subjects with bipolar disorder. The regions most affected are closely involved in processing emotions and in controlling emotional reactions. Many of these affected brain regions are part of what neuroscientists refer to collectively as the limbic system. Not all the studies agree, but several have detected decreased volume in certain brain regions called the striatum and amygdala that lie below the outer cortex or surface of the brain. The amygdala is closely associated with fear responses, rage, and other strong emotions. Parts of the striatum might be a part of the brain that is or becomes smaller than usual early in the course of bipolar disorder.

The Brain Works Differently

Other neuroimaging technologies like functional MRI, SPECT (single photon emission computed tomography), and PET (positron emission tomography) reveal not just structures but actual physiological activity in living brains. Functional imaging of the brains of people with bipolar disorder can be tricky, not only because a manic patient is unlikely to cooperate with researchers, but also because researchers need to have a very clear idea of which emotional state a patient is experiencing as her brain is being imaged. Otherwise, it is difficult to correlate the brain image with specific symptoms.

 Question

Can bipolar disorder be studied in animals?
Animals don't get bipolar disorder, but they can be used to study aspects of the illness. Medical researchers are always anxious to find or develop animal models of difficult-to-study diseases. In their search, some researchers have created a strain of genetically altered mice that needs less sleep, is more active, and responds to cocaine's rewarding effects more readily than normal mice. This is particularly interesting because lithium reduces these abnormal traits.

Despite these challenges, research has turned up some interesting clues. For example, nerve-cell activity in parts of the frontal region of the brain—the prefrontal cortex—differ with moods: brain-cell activity (indicated by increased blood flow) decreases with depression and increases with mania. Mania increases activity in the basal ganglia, deeply buried structures that include the amygdala.

Even when people with bipolar disorder are experiencing no mood episodes, their brains may reveal differences in function. Again, these differences show up in a part of the prefrontal cortex and in the amygdala. Both areas may respond more than normal when presented with an intellectual task.

Additional studies hint at some biochemical differences in the prefrontal cortex and other parts of the limbic system, including too high or too low levels of biochemicals thought to be important for maintaining the health of brain cells. Nerve-cell abnormalities would be consistent with the fact that medications like lithium and anticonvulsants control symptoms. Disturbances in neurotransmitters and hormones also might be involved. Lithium, for example, is known to interact with important chemical pathways in the brain that send signals within and between nerve cells.

Other hypotheses concentrate on problems with the functioning of neurotransmitters such as serotonin, dopamine, and norepinephrine. Imbalances in the levels of these chemical messengers could account for mood swings if, for instance, they produce too little or too much stimulation on the cellular level.

Finally, several studies report variations in the concentrations of chemicals produced by basic metabolism, suggesting there may be something wrong with the way brain cells produce or use energy.

The Challenge of Understanding Mental Disorders

Although it lingers on, the debate over nature versus nurture—or heredity versus environment—is an out-of-date concept. It is more accurate to discuss nature *and* nurture. The outside world, the environment, affects the function of the body, even going so far as to determine which genes are activated and how they function.

Essential

Distrust of psychiatry and medicine in general sometimes stems from a misunderstanding about the nature of the field. Medicine strives to have a strong scientific basis and has made significant progress toward this goal in the past hundred years, but it can't yet provide a deep understanding of the causes of many complex and serious disorders. Consequently, tests and examinations sometimes need to be redone.

Disbelief Perpetuates the Problem

Some people feel a great deal of shame regarding mental illness, considering it a sign of weakness in themselves and others. Differing opinions can be valuable, but when stubborn disbelief results in perpetuating shame and misunderstanding about what mental illness is, it can do great harm. Bipolar disorder is not simply a matter of being confused, intense, or neurotic. Decades of experience dealing with the harsh realities of this illness prove that a reliance on treatments that don't involve medication can be fatal.

Genetics and Bipolar Disorder

The evidence for a genetic predisposition to bipolar disorder is so strong that based on studies of twins, an estimated 80 percent of the risk is inherited. If one of your parents or siblings has this disorder, your chances of having it are four to ten times greater than they would be if no one in your family had it. That sounds like a huge increased risk and cause for worry, but it isn't necessarily as bad as it sounds. In fact, the numbers clearly reflect the fact that the majority (66 percent) of children who have a parent with bipolar disorder will never develop it.

Hiding in the Chromosomes

Humans have twenty-three pairs of chromosomes, the DNA-protein structures in our cells that contain all the information needed to create a human being. Genes, built into the molecular structure of DNA, encode instructions for making proteins our bodies depend on to function. From the color of your eyes to features of your personality, genes exert a tremendous—but not complete—influence on your life.

Some of these genes, like a dominant one on chromosome 11, may predispose people to illnesses like bipolar disorder. More than a dozen other chromosomal regions have been implicated as well, including a promising pair on chromosomes 6 and 8. Unfortunately, the data are still not strong enough to link bipolar disorder with any specific genes. There is no bipolar gene, just groups of genes that appear to increase the chances of developing the mood disorder. The same genes, interestingly, also appear on the list of suspected genes predisposing people to schizophrenia, major depression, and other disorders.

 Question

How soon might brain changes show up in bipolar disorder?
Perhaps as early as childhood if one MRI study is accurate. It found that the brains of children with bipolar disorder followed the same developmental pattern as the brains of children with a disorder called multidimensional impairment, which has schizophrenia- and bipolar-like symptoms. If true, this would be more evidence for common brain abnormalities underlying mood and other disorders.

Common Genes for Related Illnesses?

An example of genetic risk factors that may predispose some people to a variety of mental disorders was highlighted by a study in the United Kingdom. There, scientists identified three genetic sites that appear to increase the risk of schizophrenia. When the researchers expanded their analysis to include people with bipolar disorder, the association between one of these genetic sites and the risk of developing a mental illness became much stronger. The gene in question may control the expression of other genes.

Additional research is revealing common characteristics of families with a history of bipolar disorder. They've found, in addition to manic and depressive episodes, that obsessive-compulsive disorder occurs with bipolar disorder in some groups.

Several studies indicate that when one member of a family has bipolar disorder, the risks of another family member having bipolar disorder, schizophrenia, or schizoaffective disorder all increase. And the risk of major depressive disorder doubles in such relatives (assuming the depression is not being misdiagnosed and is really bipolar disorder). This supports the suggestion that these illnesses reflect underlying problems in the brain that may manifest themselves differently in different individuals, perhaps in concert with different inherited traits and/or exposure to different environmental factors.

The Interaction of Genes and Environment

Even if you have an identical twin—a person who shares all your genes—who develops bipolar disorder, there is a chance you will never develop the disorder. It's obvious that other factors have a very significant role in the development of this condition.

A key tenet of biological psychiatry is that because the brain is a physiological organ, mental processes have a physiological basis, a belief that goes back at least as far as Sigmund Freud. Therefore, the interplay of biology, emotions, and behavior is important for understanding the origins and nature of mental illnesses. Unfortunately, at this time scientists can't say exactly what causes bipolar disorder, nor can they explain exactly how different factors interact to produce the illness.

Stressing Cofactors

How can two people born with exactly the same genes—identical twins—develop distinct and notable differences involving, among other traits, the appearance of major mood disorders? The answer is that although they are born with identical genes, their genetic profiles don't remain identical for long. Major or minor experiences and different environmental factors affect how genes are activated and inactivated, modulated, and regulated. Experience shapes people in unique ways in combination with the genes they inherit.

 Fact

Although the underlying foundation for bipolar disorder must have been present, some people report that their episodes began when they were under great stress. These stressful events are the same ones known to threaten the health of people who don't have bipolar disorder. They include childbirth, divorce or breakup of a relationship, loss of a job, death of a loved one, and serious financial difficulties.

Just as a stressful event may trigger an initial bipolar episode, a series of stressful events may tip the balance that determines if one person predisposed to the illness goes on to develop full-blown bipolar disorder while another does not.

No Shortage of Stress

Medical researchers tend to agree that stress in a variety of forms is probably the most important trigger for bipolar disorder. Another is sleep disturbance, although it can be difficult to dissect cause from effect with this proposed trigger.

Stress can also result from other illnesses and injuries as well as from marriage and pregnancy, as discussed in the previous chapter. Some proposed stressors in this category include multiple sclerosis (MS), epilepsy, and brain injury. The finding that MS (and not the medications used to treat it) can double the risk of developing bipolar disorder supports the argument that either outside influences can affect the chance of developing bipolar disorder or that the nervous systems of people predisposed to bipolar disorder are susceptible to MS as well.

Life Experience Matters

Mental illness can develop in some people who have not been exposed to any events that others would consider traumatic. New research suggests it may also be true that traumatic events can change the brain. Post-traumatic stress, for example, may be correlated with changes in the sensitivity of neural circuits in the brain's amygdala. It is entirely feasible that traumatic events affecting children predisposed to mood disorders can trigger mental illness.

Abuse

Some studies indicate that children and adolescents who are physically or sexually abused are more likely to manifest bipolar symptoms. Obviously, the abuse does not cause bipolar disorder—if it did, many more people would suffer from this illness.

In some cases, children with bipolar disorder might be more likely to be abused by unfit parents or guardians who can't cope with the disturbing, troubling, and destructive symptoms. As a result, some children might receive excessive and unreasonable punishments from adults who lack the skills or ability to cope. But since abuse is so stressful, there can be little doubt it could trigger bipolar symptoms in someone predisposed to them.

Social Support

Lack of social support has also been connected to increased bipolar episodes. First, social support can help people deal, to a certain degree, with their problems, even problems as serious as bipolar disorder. Of course, having a shoulder to cry on will not relieve extreme symptoms like mania or depression, but having supportive friends and family nearby to lend support between episodes tends to reduce stress. And reduced stress is less likely to trigger episodes. Not having a strong support network and being socially isolated and lonely, by contrast, can only increase the likelihood of exaggerated perceptions and the stress of social isolation.

People without family and friends can make social contacts by taking advantage of support groups and mental health advocacy groups. The problems presented by isolation can also be addressed in personal and group therapy sessions.

 Alert

Though there is much evidence to suggest stressors from daily life events can trigger serious episodes, some skeptics question this assertion. For example, they argue that people might claim after the fact that a particular stress associated with daily life caused an episode, at which time some people might be looking for an excuse for their behavior.

It helps nearly everyone to have a trusted confidant to talk things over with. Also, a friend can help by reminding someone to take medication, driving him to the doctor, and reassuring him he has someone nearby to help. Not having a strong social support network can make it less likely someone will get the help he needs when a crisis threatens.

CHAPTER 6

Pharmacological Treatment for Bipolar Disorder

B ipolar disorder is a long-term illness; you should expect it to require long-term treatment. Medications, psychological counseling or psychotherapy, education, and support groups contribute to successful treatment for most people who are able to get their bipolar disorder under control.

Stages of Treatment

Your treatment might include as many as four of the following stages, but it will probably include a minimum of two: initial and continued treatment with long-term medications.

✓ Hospitalization may be necessary if you become psychotic, suicidal, or a threat to others.
✓ Initial treatment will include medications prescribed to get your moods under control as soon as possible.
✓ Maintenance treatment involves the best medication or combination of medications to keep your moods under control for the long term. This is important because if you stop taking them, bipolar episodes are almost certain to return.
✓ Substance-abuse treatment will be necessary if you are addicted to or abuse drugs, including alcohol. These substances prevent your medications from working properly

and can promote bipolar symptoms. You won't be able to manage your illness if you abuse drugs.

Short of a cure, it would be wonderful if there were one pill for everyone that relieved bipolar symptoms without side effects. The reality is it often requires a combination of medications to get control of mood episodes, but once the right combination is found, it can work well for most patients. These medicines include mood stabilizers, antipsychotics, sleep aids, antianxiety drugs, and perhaps antidepressants.

History of Treatment

Before advances in biological psychiatry lead to the development of effective or partially effective treatments for many mental disorders, doctors used talk therapy alone to treat disorders such as schizophrenia and bipolar disorder. It didn't work. As a result, patients with severe mental disorders were confined to psychiatric hospitals for years.

Essential

Sometimes symptoms attributed to bipolar disorder are caused by another serious condition. Patients with bipolar symptoms should receive a complete physical exam to exclude metabolic diseases or ailments such as Huntington's disease, brain tumors, or other medical conditions.

Electroconvulsive Therapy

Later, patients were treated with electroconvulsive therapy (ECT), a treatment in which an electric current is passed through the brain. The current briefly disrupts the brain's electrical activity and, perhaps, resets aberrant nerve circuits that contribute to symptoms. Back in the mid-twentieth century, ECT was a much more crude treatment then it is today; it got the name shock therapy. The electrical current caused the body to convulse severely, sometimes so strongly it broke bones. The treatment could wipe out memories and leave patients traumatized. ECT became a symbol in the public mind of inhumane treatment.

Although that image lingers, it has been inaccurate for many years. Much has improved since the early days of ECT. Today, a lower current is used; patients are anesthetized and given muscle relaxants; side effects are decreased. Although it is not a first choice for treating bipolar disorder, it turns out that six to twelve ECT sessions can be highly effective for treating severe, life-threatening depression and manic and mixed episodes that do not respond to medication. It can also be useful when pregnancy prevents the use of more commonly prescribed treatments. ECT may leave you with disorientation and memory loss, but these are short-term side effects.

However, it was the expanding use of lithium in the 1970s that provided the first major breakthrough in the treatment of bipolar disorder. Lithium helped turn bipolar disorder into a treatable condition.

Despite this progress, there are aspects of current treatment that could stand improvement. Some people find the right treatment, stick with it, and experience few or no side effects. They respond so well other people would not know they had the disorder. However, some people find that medication improves some symptoms more than others. Mania may fade but depression lingers, for example. Others might find that their episodes are under control, but their ability to work or maintain close relationships still suffers.

Side effects prevent some people from benefiting from otherwise effective medications. A minority of patients fail to respond to one or more medications.

TABLE 6-1: MEDICATIONS USED TO TREAT BIPOLAR SYMPTOMS

Medication	Use	Examples
Lithium	Mood stabilizer	Eskalith, Lithobid, Lithonate
Antipsychotics	Manic and mixed psychosis	First Generation: haloperidol (Haldol), chlorpromazine (Thorazine); Second Generation: olanzapine (Zyprexa), aripiprazole (Abilify), quetiapine (Seroquel), risperidone (Risperdal)
Anticonvulsant compounds	Mood stabilizers	valproate (Depakote), carbamazepine (Tegretol), lamotrigine (Lamictal), topiramate (Topamax)
Antidepressants	Depressive episodes	Bupropion (Wellbutrin); Selective serotonin reuptake inhibitors: fluoxetine (Prozac), fluvoxamine (Luvox), sertraline (Zoloft), paroxetine (Paxil), citalopram (Celexa), Monoamine oxidase inhibitors: tranylcypromine (Parnate), phenelzine (Nardil)

Despite these problems, the 80 percent or greater success rate of current treatments has made enormous differences in peoples' lives. Treatment was much worse just a few decades ago, when understanding, diagnosis, and treatment of bipolar disorder was less advanced than it is today.

 Fact

In most cases, medications for bipolar disorder are prescribed by a psychiatrist, but in some states, other professional health care providers can write prescriptions. These might be clinical psychologists or psychiatric nurses. It is important you keep anyone who writes your prescriptions informed about how well the medications are working and any side effects they produce. Also, give them a written list of every other drug, supplement, or home remedy you take to avoid adverse interactions.

Mood Stabilizers

Mood stabilizers are used to control bipolar mood swings so thoughts, behaviors, and energy levels remain healthy and relatively even. They can help manage mania as well as depression in bipolar disorder and are usually taken long term. They also are used to counter symptoms of acute mixed, manic, and hypomanic episodes. The mood stabilizers you are most likely to encounter are lithium, valproate, and carbamazepine.

These medications appear to work by interacting directly with brain cells and the chemicals they use to communicate with each other. Their effects are temporary, so they must be taken frequently, as prescribed by your doctor.

Lithium

The first effective mood stabilizer is still often used as an initial treatment to keep manic and depressive episodes under control. A simple chemical element, it is sold as lithium carbonate and lithium citrate.

 Alert

> The medication or combination of medications you and your doctor settle on for treating your bipolar disorder will be determined by the pattern of your symptoms, your reaction to them, and your medical history. Sometimes information about medications, including warnings about their side effects, changes. You can keep up with these changes by visiting the FDA website (*www.fda.gov*).

No one can say for certain exactly why lithium is so good at controlling the symptoms of bipolar disorder, but there are some intriguing clues. Recent research suggests that bipolar disorder is associated with decreased brain volume. One study found that lithium, but not valproic acid (VPA), increases the volume of gray matter, which is made up of neurons, in the brains of patients with bipolar disorder. The increases were accompanied by improvement of symptoms. VPA also improved symptoms, but without increasing brain volume. This suggests that the two medications work by different mechanisms. The findings are consistent with reports that lithium might lower the risk of developing another condition associated with decreased brain volume, Alzheimer's disease.

Other research indicates that lithium may influence the effects of an excitatory chemical in the brain called glutamate. Too much glutamate may correlate with manic symptoms, while too little might correlate with depressive symptoms. Of course, many more neurochemicals and brain pathways are involved in these complex emotional states, but lithium could exert its beneficial effects by interacting with such signaling mechanisms in the brain.

If you stop taking lithium for any reason, do it under a doctor's supervision. It must be done gradually because stopping abruptly can lead to an intense manic episode.

Always be sure your doctor and pharmacist are aware of all medications you are taking—prescription or over-the-counter, FDA-approved or natural remedies. Other medications can affect lithium levels in your blood. It is crucial to make sure you are not taking medications that will interfere with each other. Many medicines used to treat bipolar disorder besides lithium can interact unfavorably with other medicines.

Valproate or Valproic Acid

Valproic acid (VPA) was first used as an anticonvulsant, a drug used to stop seizures. This and several other anticonvulsants were found to relieve bipolar symptoms, especially in people whose moods cycle rapidly between mania and depression.

VPA, also called valproate (Depakote), can supplement or replace lithium treatment. For some people, it's as effective as lithium. Possible negative interactions with other medications should always be considered.

Carbamazepine

Carbamazepine (Epitol, Tegretol) can help about as many people as lithium or valproate, but it works best on its own subgroup of patients with bipolar disorder. Carbamazepine works well on acute mania, and somewhat less well (though still effectively) on depression associated with bipolar disorder.

 Alert

Anticonvulsant medication such as valproic acid and lamotrigine may increase thoughts of suicide and suicidal behavior in some individuals. This makes it especially important to watch for signs of depression in people taking them for bipolar disorder. It is just as important that patients do not stop taking these and other medications without the guidance of a physician.

Lamotrigine

Lamotrigine (Lamictal) is another anticonvulsant that acts as a mood stabilizer. It may control rapid cycling and mixed states better than valproate or carbamazepine. Its comparatively low side-effect profile makes it an attractive choice of medication, especially when patients fail to respond to other mood stabilizers. Unlike lithium, it doesn't require regular blood tests, but it can interact with other medicines to create serious side effects.

At least three other anticonvulsant medicines are sometimes used to stabilize moods, although it hasn't been demonstrated that they work better than other mood stabilizers: gabapentin (Neurontin), topiramate (Topamax), and oxcarbazepine (Trileptal).

Antidepressants

Your doctor may prescribe an antidepressant in addition to a mood stabilizer to prevent your mood from dipping into depression after your mania is under control. The mood stabilizer is essential because without it, antidepressants by themselves could send you back into a manic or hypomanic state. They can also increase your risk of developing rapid-cycling bipolar disorder. The chances of rapidly switching from depression to mania, hypomania, or a mixed state is less than 10 percent if a mood stabilizer and an antidepressant are taken together. Nevertheless, unless there is clear evidence that an antidepressant is effective for a patient, some psychiatrists avoid prescribing one. One recent study supported by the NIMH found that taking both an antidepressant and a mood stabilizer together didn't control symptoms for many people any better than a mood stabilizer alone.

Despite recent indications that the risks of taking antidepressants for bipolar disorder might not balance the benefits—and the fact that most guidelines advise against using them over the long term for treating bipolar depression—many psychiatrists continue to prescribe them. A subgroup of patients may respond well to antidepressants even if the overall population of people with the disorder does not. It is also possible that the studies questioning their effectiveness haven't impressed many doctors enough for them to change their prescribing habits. Each patient is different and their individual response to a medication should be considered in terms of its benefit for the individual.

When they prescribe antidepressants for bipolar symptoms, doctors are likely to prescribe bupropion hydrochloride (Wellbutrin), which affects the function of the neurotransmitters dopamine and norepinephrine, or one of a class of antidepressants called selective serotonin reuptake inhibitors (SSRIs) which, as their name implies, affect the function of the neurotransmitter serotonin.

If these don't work or if they produce unpleasant side effects, other options include monoamine oxidase inhibitors and tricyclic antidepressants. These classes of antidepressants are named on the basis of their mechanism of action or on their chemical structure.

Selective Serotonin Reuptake Inhibitors

Selective Serotonin Reuptake Inhibitors (SSRIs) are among the most frequently prescribed antidepressants for bipolar disorder. Serotonin released from nerve cells in the brain helps modulate mood. SSRIs keep serotonin from being reabsorbed once released. This increases the concentration of the neurotransmitter near its site of action in the brain. Examples of SSRIs include sertraline (Zoloft), fluvoxamine (Luvox), paroxetine (Paxil), and fluoxetine (Prozac).

Monoamine Oxidase Inhibitors

Monoamine oxidase (MAO) is an enzyme that has been linked to depression. Compounds such as phenelzine (Nardil), nefazodone (Serzone), and tranylcypromine (Parnate) inhibit MAO, and thus are called MAO inhibitors (MAOIs). MAOIs are generally prescribed when patients do not respond to SSRIs or cannot take them.

 Alert

Tyramine helps regulate blood pressure. MAOIs prevent tyramine from breaking down as it normally does. If you consume lots of tyramine while taking an MAOI, tyramine levels can build up and produce abnormally high blood pressure.

An important fact to remember if you take an MAOI is that foods high in tyramine, an amino acid, become off limits. This includes all types of cheese except cream cheese; all pickled or smoked meat, poultry, and fish; sausage and salami; chicken and beef liver; fava beans; sauerkraut; and red wine, sherry, and liquors. Other fermented products and overripe fruit should also be avoided. MAOIs inhibit the degradation of tyramine, which can affect blood pressure, so this compound can accumulate if you eat too much of it, which can be harmful.

Tricyclic Antidepressants

An older generation of antidepressants, tricyclic antidepressants (TCAs), are primarily prescribed as a second or third alternative for treating bipolar depression. They affect two types of neurotransmitters in the brain: serotonin and norepinephrine.

Examples of TCAs include amitriptyline (Elavil), desipramine (Norpramin, Pertofrane), imipramine (Tofranil), nortriptyline (Pamelor), and venlafaxine (Effexor).

Antipsychotics

Antipsychotics are most closely associated with the treatment of schizophrenia, but they are also effective for treating manic episodes and psychosis linked to bipolar disorder. They are often given along with mood stabilizers, but for shorter periods of time and always at the lowest possible effective dose, due to their potential side effects.

First-Generation Antipsychotics

Also called typical antipsychotics, these drugs were first developed in the 1950s. They are used less often than they used to be, largely because newer antipsychotics are believed to have better side-effect profiles. Still, older antipsychotic drugs can be a useful option when someone does not respond to mood stabilizers or when they cannot take other medications.

This class of medication includes haloperidol (Haldol), fluphenazine decanoate (Prolixin), thiothixene (Navane), perphenazine (Trilafon), chlorpromazine (Thorazine), and thioridazine (Mellaril).

Second-Generation Antipsychotics

Also called atypical antipsychotics, this class of medicines is the preferred choice among psychiatrists today. They are also much less likely to cause certain side effects affecting body movements. But, like all drugs, they are not free of side effects.

Clozapine (Closzaril) was the first in this category. Hailed as a breakthrough in the early 1990s, it remains a potentially good option for people who don't respond to other mood stabilizers or antipsychotic medications. With proper monitoring, the drug has proven to be very useful for select patients with mental disorders who don't respond to other antipsychotics.

 Fact

A medication called Symbyax was formulated as an acute treatment for adults with bipolar I depression and for adults whose depression is not relieved by other medications. It combines the antidepressant fluoxetine and the antipsychotic olanzapine. Its side effects mirror those of its components, and can include drowsiness, dry mouth, weight gain, increased appetite, and sexual problems.

Risperidone (Risperdal) and olanzapine (Zyprexa) are newer, popular second-generation antipsychotics. Risperidal treats a wide range of bipolar symptoms including manic or mixed episodes in combination with an antidepressant. It has been used to treat severe mania and psychosis in bipolar disorder. Like another new antipsychotic drug, aripiprazole (Abilify), olanzapine can be injected to quickly help decrease agitation during a mixed or manic episode. Both olanzapine and aripiprazole are approved for treatment of mixed and manic episodes.

Weight gain is a common problem with this class of drug and a potential threat to health, since it increases the risk of developing heart disease and diabetes. If you gain weight and experience other risk factors while taking antipsychotics, discuss your concerns with your doctor.

Quetiapine (Seroquel), like most atypical antipsychotics, is a good choice for countering the symptoms of sudden, severe episodes of mania. It was the first drug in its category to be approved specifically for treating bipolar disorder by the FDA, in 2006.

⌶ Essential

Many medications today are known by essentially outdated names. For instance, anticonvulsant medications are routinely used as mood stabilizers. And newer antipsychotic drugs are used to treat mania in bipolar disorder. As a result, some psychiatrists refer to antipsychotics as broad-spectrum psychotropics (drugs that act on the mind) to reflect their extended usefulness.

Antianxiety Drugs

Sometimes powerful typical antipsychotic drugs such as haloperidol (Haldol) or chlorpromazine (Largactil) are used during manic episodes. Other medications such as benzodiazepines can relieve relatively minor anxiety in people with bipolar or other disorders. They can also relieve agitation and insomnia present during manic phases. These drugs might help remove residual problems associated with bipolar disorder that are not improved by other medications, but they should be prescribed and used with caution, as they can be addictive.

Benzodiazepines

This group of antianxiety drugs includes diazepam (Valium), chlordiazepoxide (Librium), alprazolam (Xanax), lorazepam (Activan), triazolam (Halcion), and clonazepam (Klonopin).

They are often given to patients before major surgery, and are used to treat anxiety in general. Prescribed for short-term use only, they are effective at relieving anxiety or sleeplessness accompanying acute mania. Antianxiety agents supplement other medications used to treat basic mood-related symptoms.

Besides being addictive, benzodiazepines can cause drowsiness and memory loss. The often-cited warning not to operate heavy or complex machinery while taking these medications shouldn't be ignored. Nor should these medications be taken with alcohol or other drugs of abuse, a warning that applies to all medications used to treat bipolar disorder.

Finding the Right Medication(s)

Ideally, you and your doctor will find a way to treat all of your symptoms with a minimum number of medications that work in harmony. Finding the right combination of medications can be a trial-and-error process because individuals respond to medications differently. The process requires patience; it can take weeks or months for some medications to exert their beneficial effects and for some side effects to subside. In your search, you and your doctor will change one medication at a time. This will allow you to identify a specific drug if you are allergic to it and to determine its effectiveness compared to its side effects. Side effects often fade as your body gets used to a medication and the best dose is determined.

Some of the issues your doctor will keep in mind when prescribing medications include:

- The known interactions that occur with all bipolar medications
- Your medical history
- The known interactions that occur with other medications you take
- Regular, honest reports from you regarding your response to your medications, both improvements and side effects
- The need to treat as many symptoms as possible with the minimum use of medications

The last point refers to the goal of avoiding any medications you don't absolutely need. For example, a doctor would not prescribe two mood stabilizers or two antidepressants unless both were essential to improving your health. Doses should also be as low as possible to minimize side effects and drug interactions.

Some patients are luckier than others; they respond well to the first medication(s) they try. They still need regular checkups, but they are fortunate because their symptoms are controlled with a minimum of trial and error.

Other patients might experience harmful side effects or not respond to a certain medication, and will receive a prescription for a different drug. This alternative might require further changes in the medication regime, if, for example, it works better when combined with a different mood stabilizer than the one the patient is taking.

What to Know about Side Effects

It is reasonable to expect some side effects; all drugs have them— although that does not mean you will necessarily experience serious problems. Report all side effects to your doctor. If you develop minor side effects, he may advise you to tolerate them if they are not harming your health and they are working. If they are irritating or bothersome, you will have to compare the benefits of being tossed about by extreme mood swings with the inconvenience of the side effects.

But don't let dry mouth, for example, lead you to conclude you should go off a certain medication, if it is otherwise effective. Everyone suffers from minor malfunctions of the body sometimes, and many people adjust to permanent changes as long as they are not a threat to physical or mental health. Going off medication doesn't guarantee you will never again experience nausea or headaches. Obviously, if the side effects are serious, your doctor will adjust your medication or substitute a new one.

While many serious side effects are relatively rare, you should be aware of them. The following review also includes less serious side effects you should discuss with your doctor if you experience them. She can help you determine if they are cause for concern.

Lithium's Side Effects

This original mainstay treatment has been and continues to be well tolerated by many people with bipolar disorder. In one study, for example, nearly three-quarters of the participants continued taking lithium because of its effectiveness and lack of side effects. When they occur, common side effects can include dry mouth, restlessness, indigestion, bloating, acne, cold sensitivity, brittle hair and nails, painful muscles or joints, weight gain, frequent urination, loose stools, sleepiness, tremors, and problems thinking clearly.

 Alert

> Thyroid problems are not unusual in people with bipolar disorder. The thyroid gland helps regulate energy levels. Lithium can suppress thyroid function in some people. This condition, called hypothyroidism, has been linked to rapid cycling in bipolar disorder. You should have your thyroid hormone levels checked regularly. If a problem is detected, supplemental medications can routinely correct the imbalance.

It's important to have the level of lithium in your blood measured every six months to a year after you begin taking it on a regular basis. It rarely happens, but long-term use of lithium can damage the kidneys and thyroid and affect your heart rhythm. Make sure you keep your water and salt intake adequate and steady. Frequent checkups should prevent such problems by ensuring the medication is not only helping you but is being administered at safe levels. Your doctor should test your blood count, urine, thyroid, and electrolytes before prescribing lithium or other mood stabilizers.

Anticonvulant/Mood Stabilizers

If you take a mood stabilizer other than lithium, you may experience:

- Drowsiness
- Dizziness
- Headache
- Diarrhea
- Constipation
- Heartburn
- Mood swings
- Stuffed or runny nose or other cold-like symptoms
  Source: National Institute of Mental Health

Some potential side effects of valproate include nausea, vomiting, diarrhea, tremors, weight gain, hair loss, and a tendency to bruise easily. Having your blood count checked regularly can help you avoid more serious complications.

Women who begin taking it before age twenty should be aware that it can raise levels of testosterone, a hormone commonly associated with masculinity, in teenage girls. And it can promote the development of cysts in a woman's eggs. This polycystic ovary syndrome produces a host of unwanted side effects including disruption of the menstrual cycle, obesity, and excess body hair. Fortunately, these problems can be reversed when your doctor changes your prescription.

The third of the most popular mood stabilizers, carbamazepine, can cause dizziness, blurred vision, lack of coordination, sleepiness, nausea, vomiting, indigestion, and dry mouth, according to a recent study. It also can make birth control methods such as the pill, vaginal rings, and patches less effective, increasing the chances of unwanted pregnancy.

A different study reported that lamotrigine produced no side effects other than what turned out to be an insignificant rash, but not all rashes are insignificant. A serious rash called Stevens-Johnson syndrome is cause for special concern. It usually occurs soon after you start treatment. Although it is rare, be sure to call your doctor if you develop a new rash when using this, or any, medication. Other potential side effects of lamotrigine include nausea, headaches, dizziness, lack of muscle coordination, and both drowsiness and insomnia.

Antipsychotic medicines

These and other classes of medications all have strengths and weakness for treating different symptoms in different subgroups of people with bipolar disorder. A good psychiatrist will be familiar with the characteristics of each drug and be up to date on the latest research concerning them. This will help him select the right medicines for you when he takes your specific symptoms and history into consideration.

 Alert

Neuroleptic malignant syndrome (NMS) is a very rare but extremely serious complication of nearly all antipsychotic drugs. The symptoms include rigid muscles that prevent movement, racing heart beat, difficulty breathing, fever, and confusion. It is crucial that the patient is immediately taken to a hospital so these life-threatening symptoms can be treated.

It is always important to watch for extrapyramidal side effects (EPS), especially when taking older antipsychotics. A condition called tardive dyskinesia (TD) usually occurs after being on typical antipsychotics for very long periods of time, something that can be avoided. It involves involuntary and repetitive twisting movements of body muscles—including those of the face, limbs, and trunk. People with TD might blink, chew, or move their lips and tongue uncontrollably. This class of drugs can produce other types of movement disorders as well.

The second-generation antipsychotics are less likely to produce EPS, but they can produce metabolic effects that can be troublesome for some patients. Clozapine, olanzapine, and other related compounds, for instance, may increase the risk of diabetes and high cholesterol. Atypical antipsychotics are also known for promoting weight gain, although some (olanzapine and clozapine) are worse in this regard than others (risperidone and quetiapine). Ziprasidone and aripiprazole may produce the least amount of weight gain. When taking these medicines, it is important to regularly monitor your weight and other indicators of health including blood pressure, blood sugar, and cholesterol levels.

The first of the newer atypical antipsychotics, clozapine, has several temporary side effects, including drooling and lack of control of urinary functions. Over a long period of time, there can be significant weight gain, elevation in cholesterol and tryglycerides, and inflammation of the pancreas or heart muscle.

Perhaps the most serious side effect is a drop in the white blood-cell count, but this happens in only one out of 100 patients. Everyone taking it is required to get regular blood tests.

Quetiapine's (Seroquel) side effects include dizziness, sleepiness, dry mouth, and constipation. Olanzapine (Zyprexa) can make you sleepy, nauseated, and subject to unwanted muscle movements or activity.

Aripiprazole (Abilify) and ziprasidone (Geodon), like all medications, have their own side effects, but they are less likely to produce diabetes and weight gain.

Antidepressants and Antianxiety Agents

A popular antidepressant for treating bipolar disorder, bupropion (Wellbutrin) has side effects that include insomnia, headaches, constipation, and dry mouth. At exceptionally high levels, it has been associated with seizures. Some think it is less likely to produce mania than many other antidepressants, including SSRIs.

Many of the side effects associated with SSRIs are similar to those associated with mood stabilizers: nausea, headache, tremors, and both drowsiness and insomnia. SSRIs also may cause nervousness, sweating, dry mouth, loose bowels, and weight gain.

Probably the most widely discussed side effects of SSRIs are sexual in nature. Women experience lowered sex drive and men often have more difficulty achieving orgasm. As always, be aware of possible bad reactions when SSRIs are taken with other prescription and nonprescription drugs.

The side effects associated with MAOIs include drowsiness and insomnia as well as nervousness, weight gain, transient low blood pressure, and sexual problems. Moreover, MAOIs combined with decongestants or other antidepressants can produce high blood pressure. In extreme cases, this can lead to a hypertensive crisis, which in turn can cause stroke or heart attack.

Benzodiazepines, the antianxiety medications, are generally safe when taken for short periods of time. You may feel drowsy, uncoordinated, and forgetful if you experience their side effects.

Working with Your Doctor

After you have been diagnosed with bipolar disorder, it is best to work with your doctor to help get your mood swings under control. You will not help yourself if you hide anything from your doctor, fail to take your medicine, or sabotage treatment by drinking alcohol and/or abusing illegal drugs.

Patient and Healer

Having thoughts, feelings, or bodily sensations you think are embarrassing are not embarrassing to a psychiatrist. Instead, they can provide important clues about your state of health; they can guide her to prescribe the best medicines and psychotherapy for you. If, for example, you still experience uncontrollable rages in the evening and feel guilty or ashamed by them in the morning, your doctor won't judge you; she'll realize that your treatment needs to be changed. It may get easier to work with your doctor as you become more familiar with her. You will always be the patient, but if you take an active part in your treatment, you also become part of the healing team rather than an indifferent or passive medically treated bystander.

Mind and Body

Sometimes, the perceived presence of a mental disorder overshadows the presence of a physical disorder. (In fact, the distinction is misleading; mental disorders are brain diseases with real, physical bases.) This is a problem because heart disease and diabetes kill two to three times more people with mental disorders than those without mental disorders. Some of the increased illness and death among people with bipolar disorder can be traced to their greater use of tobacco than the general public. Sometimes a person with a disease like bipolar disorder may be too distracted or incapacitated by his symptoms to look after his health. A few mental health care workers may tend to see only mental problems when treating a patient and not look closely for other threats to his health. Finally, some medications used to treat bipolar disorder can increase the risk of developing health problems.

Essential

Just because you have found a good psychiatrist doesn't mean you won't need further medical care. You will still need to have a good general practitioner or primary care physician to give you yearly physical exams and deal with nonpsychiatric illnesses.

Some friends may try to give you medical advice. Listen politely, but be sure to get a professional opinion and the best medical care you can find and afford before you follow the advice of someone who is untrained and has little or no knowledge of medical practice or literature. Learn as much as you can from reputable sources that report tested medical findings. Hearsay, opinions, or religious and philosophical arguments do not treat mental disorders that have a basis in the chemistry and structure of the brain.

CHAPTER 7

Psychotherapy and Other Methods for Dealing with Bipolar Disorder

An overwhelming majority of people with bipolar disorder credit medications as the key factor that enabled them to regain control of their moods and their lives. But there are other important steps people can take to improve their lives. Most guidelines, in fact, stress the importance of patients learning about their illness (psychoeducation) to help them understand what they are experiencing. Effective therapy sessions can help people develop skills to manage the disease, understand the importance of adhering to a treatment plan, avoid or control lingering symptoms, and free themselves of guilt and negative thinking.

When Medication Is Not Enough

While medication is the basis for successful treatment, it only provides a foundation for rebuilding a life disrupted by uncontrollable mood swings. There are other important questions you will need to address.

Understanding and accepting your past is one example. Medication cannot erase the complicated feelings related to bipolar disorder; for example, embarrassment and regret over things you did and people you hurt or drove away, and feelings of shame dealing with the stigma many people still associate with mental illness.

A therapist can help you and your loved ones accept the diagnosis and benefit from it. Many people react with relief at being told they have bipolar disorder—they finally have an explanation for all the incomprehensible things that have happened in their lives. Others might respond with disbelief and need time and counseling to accept the diagnosis and benefit from it. In both instances, there is a period of adjustment as the reality of medication, regular check-ups, and other special needs become part of a new life, for the rest of that life.

Acceptance

Acceptance also means accepting the possibility of future episodes. Understanding bipolar disorder means understanding it is something that does not go away. A favorable response to medication means nothing if a patient stops treatment. Some patients do not respond to medication as well as others, and find their symptoms diminish but return periodically. While it is possible to minimize such recurrences, it is still necessary to learn to deal with the prospect of experiencing them, something that good psychotherapy can provide.

Everyone needs some level of self-confidence to live a content and fulfilled life. Receiving a diagnosis of bipolar disorder is a serious matter and should be viewed as an opportunity to recover and, eventually, flourish without the burden of mania and depression. Many people with bipolar disorder accomplish extraordinary things; many also live average and fulfilling lives. Even if someone is somewhat limited in what they can do (even with the aid of medication), she still has the possibility of pursuing worthwhile activities and building a life free of uncontrolled excessive mood fluctuations.

For many people, medications are necessary but not sufficient to get control of bipolar symptoms and associated feelings; some type of therapy can fill the gap. Repeated experience has shown that the basic treatments for bipolar disorder include medications, individual, group, or family psychotherapy, and/or education and support groups.

Finding the Right Therapy

More than one study has shown that therapy and medication are better than either treatment alone. Modern psychotherapy is much more straightforward and effective than it was years ago. Even it you don't like the idea of psychotherapy, you will probably be surprised if you investigate what it can offer today. It's important to recognize that there are different kinds of therapy, not just different styles depending on the individual therapist, but different schools of thought on how to best treat patients.

 Fact

A therapist should be a mental health professional: a licensed psychologist, counselor, or social worker, for example. He should work in concert with your psychiatrist to make sure treatment is progressing. The type of therapy, frequency, and the course of treatment will depend on your individual needs.

Some types of psychotherapies that have been helpful are:

- Cognitive behavioral therapy
- Interpersonal and social rhythm therapy
- Family-focused therapy
- Psychoeducation
- Group therapy

Cognitive Behavioral Therapy

Feelings and thoughts are intimately related. From the cognitive perspective, behavior and emotion are products of thoughts. People make certain choices in their daily lives on the basis of what they perceive about life or themselves. If people tend to do destructive things—if they are easy to anger, for example, or do not permit themselves much pleasure—then their thoughts and beliefs need to be changed. Patients in cognitive therapy are therefore encouraged to look at situations in their lives with a fresh perspective.

Essential

Progress is apparent in CBT when you start to genuinely respond differently to situations that in the past evoked a negative response or feeling. When something no longer upsets you the way it once did because you have learned to think about it differently, unproductive behavioral patterns can be broken.

Many people could benefit from cognitive behavioral therapy (CBT) because it aims to replace negative, self-defeating thought patterns and behaviors with positive ones. It teaches specific techniques and approaches for identifying and handling stressful and emotionally trying situations. A popular choice for patients with bipolar disorder, it can help you recognize and manage potential mood-episode triggers. CBT plus medication has been shown to decrease the frequency and duration of bipolar episodes and hospital admissions.

Anyone with deeply ingrained negative assumptions about himself and others might benefit from cognitive therapy.

Interpersonal and Social Rhythm Therapy

Interpersonal and social rhythm therapy (IPSRT) was created specifically to treat bipolar disorder.

It concentrates on improving relationships with others and organizing or managing daily routines, including sleep schedules, in ways that decrease the chances of manic episodes.

Since lack of sleep and disrupted daily rhythms can trigger or worsen the severity of mood episodes, IPSRT encourages patients to establish and maintain regular eating, sleeping, working, and relaxing routines while improving skills for interacting with others. One technique this individual therapy relies on is self-monitoring.

Like cognitive behavioral therapy, IPSRT in conjunction with medications has been shown to reduce bipolar disorder symptoms and increase days dominated by normal moods. By training people to adhere to medication, better handle their interpersonal relationships, and adopt regular daily routines, the therapy can have many positive effects. Over the two-year period of one study, this approach reduced the likelihood of mood episodes and increased the amount of time between them in bipolar I patients, who have the most severe symptoms. This response was particularly evident in patients free of other long-term medical problems such as heart disease or diabetes.

Question

How was a psychotherapy created especially for people with bipolar disorder?
Researchers at the University of Pittsburgh School of Medicine, like other researchers, looked at the symptoms of bipolar disorder as the result of a genetic predisposition. They went on to propose that this predisposition can result in an inability to maintain healthy sleep-wake cycles and daily rhythms. These disturbances, in turn, result in bipolar symptoms. The researchers developed IPSRT to counter the effects of these disrupted daily rhythms and demonstrated its value in patients with bipolar I, the most severe form of the disease.

There is a possibility it may even decrease suicidal thoughts and attempts in people who are particularly prone to them. One indication of its potential usefulness is the observation that people who drop the therapy have an increased risk of relapsing into mood episodes. Its value lies in preventing episodes more than in speeding recovery from them.

Another type of therapy shown to be effective for treating bipolar disorder is called intensive clinical management therapy. It includes discussion of the possible causes, symptoms, and treatments of bipolar disorder.

Family-Focused Therapy

Bipolar symptoms often disrupt family life and generate great stress in a home. And yelling, arguing, anger, and distrust in a home make it much more difficult for someone with bipolar disorder to gain control over the illness. Family-focused therapy has been shown to help.

Unlike individual therapies (like those discussed above), family-focused therapy sessions include family members as well as the patient. It teaches family members how to better deal with one another and the illness, how to spot the beginning of new mood episodes, and how to best help their loved one. Successful family therapy can lower stress levels in a home and decrease the impact and occurrence of conflicts.

Like all forms of therapy, it is provided along with medications and has been demonstrated in controlled studies to help patients and their close relatives by decreasing relapses.

 Fact

Family psychoeducation and other therapies have been shown repeatedly to help people cope with bipolar disorder and regain control of their lives. Many regions of the country, unfortunately, lack enough qualified, trained therapists to provide help to everyone who wants or needs it. Ask your health care provider, contact the organizations that promote mental health awareness (listed at the end of this book), and ask members of support groups where good therapists can be found.

Psychoeducation

Several studies conducted in Spain showed that people who attended programs that educated patients about bipolar disorder had fewer recurrences over two years. It helped them maintain regular lifestyles, which are less likely to promote mood episodes, and it enabled them to spot symptoms early, which in turn allowed them to seek treatment and head off or limit episodes.

Learning more about bipolar disorder, its treatment, and its impact offers significant advantages over limiting treatment to taking pills and hoping they will do the job. Reading this and other books on the subject is part of psychoeducation. Learning about the illness under the guidance of a qualified expert can offer information especially relevant to your situation, even if sessions are offered in a group setting. Patients and their families can help themselves by taking advantage of psychoeducation programs.

Spotting specific triggers that lead to relapses and recognizing warning signs that an episode is about to start provides a sense of control over the illness; it enables you to seek early treatment to minimize the frequency, length, and severity of episodes.

Obviously, it helps to know what's going on with a condition that has such a tremendous impact on your life. Learn all you can so you can take charge and control it to the fullest extent of your ability. Don't be passive when dealing with this or any other threatening health problem.

Group Therapy

Group therapy usually consists of a small number of people with a particular condition or goal in common. For example, a therapy group may be made up of people with just bipolar disorder or major depressive disorder or people with mood disorders or many different disorders.

It provides a chance for people to talk to and learn from others who are facing similar challenges and dealing with similar problems. This process can help people improve their skills relating to others.

A therapist guides or facilitates the sessions, posing questions and suggesting group exercises. The therapist also tries to elicit communication among group members. Patients can make suggestions to each other, question one another, and speak plainly about their impressions of themselves and others. It is the group therapist's responsibility to make sure these discussions are productive and helpful. Group therapy, as well as support groups discussed later, can be helpful in general and particularly if someone has trouble relating to other people.

Essential

No single psychotherapy works for all people with bipolar disorder. The choice of therapy should depend on your needs and circumstances. A particular individual therapy and/or family or group therapy may be best at one time, while another type of therapy may be more helpful if circumstances change. For instance, studies suggest that patients with bipolar disorder and anxiety may respond better to intensive clinical management therapy while patients with bipolar disorder but no other medical problems may respond better to IPSRT.

Not all trials show a benefit of psychotherapy for treating acute cases of bipolar disorder, but enough support the recommendation that medication be combined with therapy to provide the best treatment now available.

One of the largest treatment studies ever conducted on bipolar disorder was the NIMH-funded Systematic Treatment Enhancement Program for Bipolar Disorder clinical trial. It demonstrated that patients who received medication and nine months of either family-focused, cognitive behavior, or interpersonal and social rhythm therapy were more likely to recover from episodes sooner and remain healthy longer. Furthermore, the results showed that participants stuck to their treatment plans better, had fewer relapses, and required fewer hospitalizations than medicated patients who had just three sessions of psychoeducation.

For others, occupational therapy or vocational training might also prove useful. This provides training (and sometimes certification) in a particular career. If you need to learn a new or different kind of job skill, or have been out of work for some time but would like to try again, you might consider vocational training. There are many public and private programs available to teach people new job skills.

Diet and Exercise

Poor physical health may require a person to take medications that interfere with bipolar disorder medicines. The stress of poor health might also create discomfort that can contribute to symptoms. Keeping in shape eliminates many possible problems for everyone, not just people with bipolar disorder. Besides avoiding drugs and alcohol, diet and exercise are two of the most straightforward ways to increase your odds of regaining and maintaining health.

Diet

It is unrealistic for most people to try to live without any guilty indulgences when it comes to food. Moreover, for the person with bipolar disorder, a fanatical eating lifestyle can be associated with undesired behavior. It is best to avoid extremes, even when it comes to diet and nutrition.

 Fact

When rebuilding your life after suffering years of symptoms, pay attention to your physical and mental health. Running, for example, has been reported to ease the symptoms of depression. Other exercises have benefits, as well. Getting well can mean more than simply finding the right medication and therapist. While medication makes recovery possible, a healthy diet and exercise increase your ability to cope with stress and decrease your chances of developing health problems that can complicate recovery.

You don't need to be a licensed nutritionist to eat well. Check with your doctor to find out if she has any recommendations specifically for you. It is possible to get all the nutrients experts recommend by eating moderately and eating food that isn't processed and packaged (and laden with sugars and fat as main ingredients). Obviously, you won't be able to avoid all processed foods, but the more you make basic foods like vegetables, fruits, whole grains, lean meats, poultry, and well-chosen varieties of fish the basis of your diet, the easier it will be to avoid obesity and other problems linked to the modern American diet.

Fortunately, food products have nutritional information on their labels. Pay attention to how many servings there are. Some food producers try to fool consumers by taking, say, a small amount of food and dividing it up into ten servings. Thus, a food that contains 1,000 calories when eaten in its entirety is made to look as if it only has 100 calories.

 Alert

It can be very difficult to eat even moderately well. Supermarkets and much of the food industry are heavily tilted toward processed foods. Just compare the number and variety of cookies and chips in a typical supermarket to the number of fresh, unprocessed foods offered. It takes time to make the transition to eating better; you don't have to change all at once. Approach the goal slowly but steadily without self-imposed pressure. If you persist, you may significantly decrease your chances of becoming or remaining overweight and developing associated health risks.

Again, moderation is a useful guide. Watch out for sugar in all its variations; for example, rice syrup, corn syrup, high fructose corn syrup, sucrose, glucose, etc.

Avoid foods with more than 30 percent total fat. Limit saturated fats (often found in animal products) and try to go with monounsaturated fats (found in nuts like walnuts, almonds, and pistachios and in avocados). Avoid foods with coconut oil, palm oil, and palm kernel oil; look for olive and canola oil instead.

And don't torture yourself if you have some junk food once in a while, even once a week. It is better to limit your intake of junk food to, say, once a week than to give up after giving into temptation once and reverting to the typical American diet.

Exercise

You don't have to join a fitness club or gym to exercise, and you don't need to take a formal class or take part in a competitive sport to get exercise. Walking is exercise. A half hour per day can improve your heart rate, muscle tone, and disposition. If you take public transportation, get on and off a stop or two early to add a few more minutes of walking to your day. You can park a short distance from your destination, if it is safe, whenever you drive somewhere. Being in the fresh air and sunshine—even in cold weather—can have positive effects on depression, and can sometimes have a calming effect on hyperactivity.

Perhaps the single most important factor in finding a workable exercise regime is picking something you enjoy doing and changing your routine often. It is not likely that you continue exercising if you don't enjoy it, particularly if you are easily distracted.

Support Groups

Adjusting to the reality of bipolar disorder can be easier if you have reminders that you are not alone. Attending support-group meetings is an obvious way to do this. Besides being in an atmosphere where you don't have to worry about being "different," you can share stories with others that might comfort, inform, or inspire. You may also find some people you enjoy sharing time with outside the group.

Support Groups for Bipolar Disorder

Your doctor, hospital, and public library are some of the resources you might contact for finding a nearby support group that deals exclusively with bipolar disorder. The Depression and Bipolar Support Alliance is another great resource. Visit the DBSA website at *www.dbsalliance.org*.

Groups focused specifically on bipolar disorder are normally run by a trained facilitator and can take three basic forms:

- **Groups solely for people with bipolar disorder:** The main purpose of a support group is to provide hope and understanding based on shared needs and experiences; its goal is not necessarily altering thoughts or behavioral patterns, which is the purpose of therapy. In fact, you shouldn't expect a trained therapist to be present; the members of the group might take turns leading the meeting.
- **Groups for family and friends:** This type of group allows people to share thoughts and feelings about how the illness affects them. They can also trade tips and recommendations for building trust and understanding between a person with bipolar disorder and family members.
- **Groups for both people with bipolar disorder and their loved ones:** They offer the opportunity to share experiences and give and receive advice from different standpoints.

If you can't find a support group or don't feel comfortable with those you can find, consider starting your own. You doctor or therapist may be able to offer some suggestions and even refer some potential members who can contact you if they are interested.

Alternative and Nontraditional Approaches

After she began to benefit from treatment, Emma Parker Bowles wrote, "There are so many routes to go down, be it holistic, counseling, alternative therapies or prescription medication. I am doing a combination of all of the above and it feels like there is light where it once was dark."

Non-mainstream approaches fall into two categories: things you think and things you swallow; neither should be dismissed outright nor accepted wholeheartedly. You shouldn't swallow everything some people want you to think, and you shouldn't think that everything some people suggest you swallow will work.

Spirituality

Spirituality has many meanings. It can refer to a religious belief and it can refer to a loosely structured, nondenominational philosophy. It can also refer to an attitude—a conviction or belief that you have a definite reason for living. Some people feel spiritual while enjoying nature, listening to music, or meditating.

Whatever form it takes, it will not cure or control bipolar illness, but a spiritual orientation that satisfies your needs might give you strength to help you deal with this disorder. Perhaps you feel that the mood disorder that has so impacted your life has to be about something more than genes and that, in some deep way, there is a reason you have to deal with it.

 Alert

If spirituality is important for you, it is essential that you integrate it into your treatment plan along with medications and therapy. There is nothing wrong with believing in a power or powers greater than humankind; it can be a source of great strength and reassurance. Many organized religions or informal spiritual practices are accommodating to the realities of mental disorders, but some are not. Make sure you pursue a course that offers all the best treatments you and your doctor can find because you need them when dealing with this disorder.

Avoid spiritual groups or practices that claim that mental disorders can be "cured" through nonmedical means. This includes mental exercises, strong prayer, faith healing, exorcising demons, atoning for sins, or working through karma. There is no evidence that any of these work, while there are volumes of evidence that medication and psychotherapy improve symptoms for the majority of people. Unproven alternative treatments that promise a cure are unethical and can lead to unfortunate consequences when the patient not only suffers a relapse but is made to feel weak or ashamed for having failed.

While there are instances that support the notion that we live in an overly medicated society, the treatment of serious mood disorders is not one of them. When people are convinced that medications should be discarded in favor of prayer alone or other approaches, the results can be tragic.

Supplements and Manipulations

Compared to studies indicating the benefits of medications and psychotherapy for treating bipolar disorder, alternative treatments have very little scientific support. That is not to say some may not have benefits; it's just that no one has tested them or they have never demonstrated effectiveness in controlled experiments.

Some people believe, for example, that omega-3 fatty acids might ease depressive symptoms and improve moods because populations that eat lots of fish may have fewer cases of bipolar disorder. No one has yet shown, however, that the fatty acids actually improve health in people with the disorder. There is a difference between a possible lower incidence of illness and effective treatment. Omega-3s have been shown to improve cardiovascular health. Future studies might change the status of this supplement with regard to bipolar disorder.

St. John's Wort has been reported to aid depression, but this claim has been called into question by recent studies. It has the potential to interact with other medications, and the staff at the Mayo Clinic warns that it also potentially triggers manic episodes in select individuals. The same warning is applied to an amino acid used as a supplement, S-adenosyl-L-methionine (SAMe). Also thought to help with depression, there is no evidence it can control mood episodes.

There is no proof yet that Chinese medications or herbal remedies are effective in the treatment of bipolar illness. Someday there may be, but until then, keep in mind that the side effects and potential interactions of these untested materials are largely unknown.

Other alternative treatments come with fewer caveats and warnings. They aren't cures, of course, and they may or may not relieve bipolar symptoms—there is no evidence they do—but they may have other benefits such as relaxing you, easing aches, or relieving stress.

 Alert

> If you decide to add alternative approaches to your treatment regimen, be sure to tell your health care providers. Keep taking your medications and seeing your therapist. Watch out for interactions with your medications. Keep track of your feelings and moods. Additional therapies are only good if they do not harm, improve your life in some way, reduce your stress, and make it easier for you to function.

Acupuncture uses very thin needles to simulate points in the body defined by ancient Chinese medicine. The theory is the inserted needles correct the flow of energy through the body. Acupuncture has been shown to have some proven positive effects, but not yet for the treatment of bipolar disorder, although some claim it may be effective in some cases of depression. It won't interfere with bipolar medication. If you try it, be sure your acupuncturist uses antiseptic procedures and sterilized needles.

Yoga is a name applied to many different styles of an effective stress-reducing, flexibility-enhancing, and spiritually invigorating practice with origins in India. Some styles of yoga stress physical movements, akin to a Pilates class. Other versions combine movement with breathing exercises and meditation. Doctors at the Mayo Clinic say it might ease depression and mood swings. Its emphasis on centering, calming thoughts, stress reduction, and gradual physical improvement is believed to offer many health benefits.

Massage therapy provides a more passive route to physical relaxation and stress relief. Anything that safely and effectively relieves anxiety and stress is good for helping someone control bipolar symptoms.

Getting Help with Other Problems

You might feel very optimistic when you respond well to medication or when your family and friends are supportive and understanding. But having bipolar disorder can still cause problems, no matter how effective medication is, and things that have no connection to bipolar can—and will—go wrong. Surprisingly, even excessively good news can present problems. For example, parties and celebrations can set in motion mood instability or feelings of grandiosity in some people.

Dealing with Loss

A major loss, such as that of a loved one through death or divorce, or loss of a job, can increase the risk of depression or sometimes even mania. Depending on the nature of the loss, there might also be a tendency to become overly involved in other people's lives. Some might tend toward seeking comfort through inappropriate sex.

There are three main sources you can turn to when dealing with profound loss. The first is professional support. Ask for help. Would more or different counseling, therapy, or medication be appropriate?

 Fact

Some doctors estimate that between 50 and 70 percent of the appointments made with primary care physicians do not have a significant physical basis. Instead, the complaints or ailments seem to be psychological in origin—people dealing with discontent, loss, or personal crises in relatively ineffective ways.

If you are seeing a therapist, request an extra session if you feel it would help. If you start engaging in behavior that is associated with a symptom of bipolar disorder—such as radically changing eating or sleeping patterns, spending lots of money, or having random and excessive sex—you need to inform your health care provider(s).

There is also personal support. If you are lucky enough to have a significant support system, it can be a valuable resource. It might consist of family, friends, a support group, or a combination of them. Talk in confidence to people you trust. If others are touched by the loss you are experiencing, listen to them discuss how it has affected them. Remember that the people in your support network have their own feelings, needs, and responsibilities. Also, avoid getting overly gossipy about whatever just happened. If you have obsessive thoughts about what other people did or should be doing, share them with your doctor.

A third resource is self-support. If you have developed some type of personal philosophy or spiritual foundation, you might be able to tap into it even before your mood spirals down. Loss is a part of life. Make an effort to use the inner reserves and strength you built up during your recovery to cope with crises as they come along.

Dealing with Gain

Many people fear change, even positive change. Often, it seems safer to keep things as they are, so people sometimes turn down major opportunities to avoid making a dramatic adjustment. For people who have found a daily routine that works for them, new opportunities can be very unsettling. Moving to a new area can mean having to find new doctors, acquaintances, and friends. It can mean finding a place to live, shop, work, and play. A job promotion or increase in finances can mean new responsibilities that complicate life. Major changes like these can increase the risk of a depressive or manic episode.

If you are succeeding professionally or if someone important has come into your life, the same basic strategies should be employed. Tell your doctor(s) how this new development is making you think and behave. Remember that loss and sadness will come your way again—that neither good news nor bad news lasts forever. Feel deserving of your good fortune, but remind yourself there are other good people who deserve good fortune, too.

CHAPTER 8

What Happens
Without Treatment?

If everyone who has bipolar disorder could receive the right medical treatment for their manic and depressive symptoms, the disorder itself would be much less of a problem than it is. Unfortunately, some people never receive the right medical treatment—and some never receive any treatment.

Suicide and Bipolar Disorder

Many people do not realize that suicide is one of the leading causes of death, both in the United States and around the world. Estimates for the percentages of people with bipolar disorder who kill themselves range from 10 to 20 percent, with 15 percent the most commonly cited figure. Sixty percent of people with bipolar disorder who commit suicide were abusing drugs or alcohol when they took their lives.

 Fact

More than 45 percent of people with bipolar disorder attempt suicide. Suicide attempts are more common early in the course of the illness and most likely when a person is depressed or experiencing a mixed episode showing signs of depression and mania.

Global Suicide Rates

The World Health Organization (WHO) has compiled some alarming figures about suicide. It estimates that around 1 million people each year, or 3,000 per day, take their own lives. This is more than die as a result of war and homicide combined. Among people under age twenty-five, it is one of the top three causes of death. The staggering size of the numbers reflects the 60 percent increase in suicide rates since 1965. By the end of the next decade, 1.5 million people per year are expected to kill themselves.

Sixty percent of suicides occur in Asia, where cultural factors make impulsive acts of desperation more common. Still, many die as a consequence of mental illness.

Suicide in the United States

In the United States, about 33,000 people commit suicide a year. It is the eleventh leading cause of death across age groups. Although experts estimate there are between one and two dozen suicide attempts for every suicide death, more people die by suicide each year than die as a result of homicide.

Essential

Call for help! The National Suicide Prevention Lifeline is available for everyone. Call if you need help or if someone you know needs help. It is confidential and available every day year round, 24 hours a day. Call toll-free 1-800-273-TALK (8255).

About four times as many males than females die of suicide, though females are more likely to attempt it. The method used seems to account for some of the difference. Firearms account for about 56 percent of the suicides by males and only 31 percent of suicides by women. Women resort more often to poisoning (40 percent) compared to men (13 percent). Suffocation accounts for similar percentages in the two sexes: 23 percent for males and 19 percent for females.

Other Risk Factors

Besides suicide, a person with untreated bipolar disorder is potentially vulnerable to other troubling scenarios. There is an association between severe, untreated mental illness in general and violence. When violence is committed by someone who is ill, the victim is most often a family member. However, the overwhelming majority of people with mental illnesses are not violent. In fact, due to conditions such as homelessness, they are more likely to be victims of a crime than perpetrators of it.

 Fact

> On February 7, 2001, an untreated patient with bipolar disorder fired several shots at the White House before being wounded in the knee by the Secret Service. A former West Point cadet, he had been fired from his job at the IRS and claimed the government was persecuting him. President Bush was not at the White House at the time.

The Truth about Mental Illness and Violence

There is a lot of misunderstanding regarding the tendency of people with mental disorders to commit crimes, much of it perpetrated by lurid news accounts. The NIMH surveyed nearly 18,000 people with various mental illnesses and found that people with schizophrenia, major depression, or bipolar disorder were two to three times more likely to assault someone. While 7 percent of people with no mental illness were violent, 16 percent of those with serious mental illness were. The greatest threat is posed by people with serious mental illness who abuse drugs and alcohol—nearly 44 percent of them were violent. Compare this to the fact that 35 percent of people who abuse alcohol and drugs but have no mental illness are nevertheless violent at some point in their lives. As Richard A. Friedman, MD, concluded in an article in the *New England Journal of Medicine*: "The challenge for medical practitioners is to remain aware that some of their psychiatric patients do in fact pose a small risk of violence, while not losing sight of the larger perspective—that most people who are violent are not mentally ill, and most people who are mentally ill are not violent."

When someone with bipolar disorder does become violent, it is usually linked to substance abuse and the effects of a serious manic, depressive, or mixed episode.

In addition to suicide and violence, there are a number of general risks associated with bipolar disorder if it is not treated. For example, in an effort to deal with their problems, close to one in two people with bipolar disorder have used alcohol or illegal drugs. This can of course lead to heightened bipolar symptoms—and the many troubling behaviors that go along with them.

Also, despite the boastfulness that often accompanies mania, many people with untreated bipolar disorder are unable to take care of themselves as independent adults. They can end up homeless, living in poverty, or under the guardianship of an uncaring person.

There is also the sheer waste of life: People with bipolar disorder might lose as many as nine years from their lives due to the general abuse they undergo as a result of their illness. They can lose as many as twelve years of health and fourteen years of productivity. Besides dealing with episodes, untreated bipolar disorder can cost people valuable time trying to put their lives back in order after a major episode.

How Loved Ones Are Affected

As a person with bipolar disorder spirals out of control, friends and family might feel as though they have lost him, since the person they used to know does not seem to be there anymore. Even though someone with bipolar disorder may have a fair amount of time between episodes, there is always the fear that another episode is coming. Others start to keep their distance in anticipation of the coming bad times. Once again, they end up missing the person they used to know.

This sense of loss can be especially troubling when an ill person otherwise has a creative and engaging personality. A young protégé, for example, might feel deeply pained having to sever ties with a mentor whose teaching she appreciated and whose company she enjoyed, but she just could not take the mentor's mood swings anymore.

Loss of Sleep, Time, and Energy

Some people may find their lives are at the mercy of someone's bipolar symptoms. Being awakened at odd hours, having to listen to someone, or drive him someplace or bail him out of jail becomes a full-time job. Sometimes, people end up canceling other social or professional plans in order to take care of the latest crisis.

Depression can be as time-consuming for a caregiver as mania. A caregiver may go out of her way to spend time with or do errands or favors for the ill person in hopes it will ease burdens and aid recovery. And, of course, caregivers and friends can spend a significant amount of time and effort worrying, enough sometimes to threaten their own health and well-being.

Loss of Money

There are many ways a person with bipolar disorder can cause a loved one to lose money. Maybe she will simply take it, or invest it in a sure-to-fail scheme. Also, some people might borrow small and large sums of money after having spent or lost all of theirs. Or, if they are unable to hold down a job, they might ask to borrow money because they need to eat or pay the rent.

In other instances, a person with bipolar disorder might ask for financial assistance to get out of trouble that can be traced to the illness. Maybe he needs to be bailed out of jail, pay a fine, or make restitution.

When the depressive side of bipolar disorder strikes, others might spend money on the affected person in order to cheer him up. Or maybe they just want to make sure he is eating and attending to other basic needs. Many people find that being close to someone with untreated bipolar disorder is expensive.

Loss of Direction

If someone spends a great deal of his life caring for or worrying about someone with this illness, he might find his own accomplishments and sense of satisfaction limited. The goals and plans of the caregiver may fade as he instead tries to save or protect the person he looks after. A person with bipolar disorder can take over a caregiver's life if the caregiver does not protect himself.

Children of an untreated parent are likely to be denied basic nurturing and socialization that help ensure a successful life. Such children might grow up with very little sense of security about life, because from one moment to the next they never knew what their parent was going to be like.

 Question

Clearly, untreated bipolar disorder can have crippling emotional effects, but are there also negative physical effects?
More than one study has found changes in brain structure associated with this mood disorder. It is still too early, however, to figure out exactly which brain regions contribute most to the illness. The overall conclusion of the studies completed so far is that people with bipolar disorder are more likely to have significant changes in the volume of their brains compared to people who don't have this mood disorder. Unfortunately, the observed changes cannot be used to diagnose the condition.

A relative might be insulted, belittled, bullied, yelled at, laughed at, or face a combination of unpleasant verbal assaults when dealing with someone in the throes of a manic episode.

When depression takes over, the loved one may feel the burden of sadness that pervades the household. The caregiver might begin to feel guilty for not being able to do enough to help.

A tragic element of such situations is that the person with the disorder might be a good and kind person whose unpleasantness is not the result of a conscious decision but rather a natural manifestation of the illness. Obviously, lack of treatment can damage not only the person with the mood disorder, but also those close to him. However, sometimes the reasons for not getting treatment are complicated.

When Patients Accept Diagnosis but Treatment Fails

Psychiatrists estimate that the treatment success rate for bipolar disorder is an impressive 80 percent. But what about the other 20 percent? While some of these people are willing to accept a doctor's diagnosis, for one reason or another, their treatment fails.

Side Effects of Medication

Some cases of noncompliance—not taking the prescribed medications—are undoubtedly due to unpleasant side effects. Often, this excuse is understandable when the side effects include problems such as severe nausea. In a few cases, patients might exaggerate side effects, imagine them, or even lie about them.

Regardless of how or why it happens, the effect is the same: Some patients stop taking their medications. It is not unusual for a doctor and her patient to try several different treatment regimens before finding one that works. In some cases, however, patients might give up. They might risk the problems associated with mania and depression rather than deal with real or imagined side effects they fear. This attitude, unfortunately, does not consider the damage repeated mood swings can produce or the possibility that future episodes might be worse than any experienced so far.

Despite the trouble it takes to find a good combination of medications, it will pay off if you stick with it and work with your doctor. Experience has shown that living without any medication is likely to be the most dangerous alternative for the majority of patients.

Finding the Right Combination

Bipolar disorder includes both mania and depression. There also can be other complications that signal a need for sleep aids and/or antipsychotic or antianxiety medication. Unfortunately, sometimes one medication can react negatively with another, causing harmful side effects. Or maybe a patient does not respond to one mood stabilizer, so another is tried . . . and this new one does not work well with an antidepressant.

If many but not all symptoms are under control, you and your doctor must decide whether to let things be or substitute different medications. It can involve trial and error because every person is unique. However, psychiatrists continue to learn more about what works and what doesn't, making your chances of eventually finding some helpful combination of medications better than it was just years ago.

Additional Disorders

Some people have both bipolar disorder in addition to schizophrenia, or attention deficit hyperactivity disorder, or some other mental health problem. The task of finding an effective combination of medications in such situations may be more challenging, and the likelihood of having complicating side effects increases.

Moreover, one doctor may diagnose bipolar and schizophrenia in one patient while another might conclude the patient has only a mood disorder. The second doctor may order more tests and change the medication regimen. This will increase the time until an effective course of treatment is found. Unfortunately, this can be part of the process because there are no clinical tests for bipolar disorder. Proper diagnosis and treatment depends on patient history, the psychiatrist, and the response of the individual patient.

No Response to Medication/Misdiagnosis

A minority of people with bipolar disorder, around 20 percent, either do not respond to medication or stop responding to it after a while. An assortment of other medications may be tried, but in some cases, nothing seems to be effective. In other cases, medications may control mania but not depression, or vice versa.

While some patients persist longer than others in trying to find medications that work, others reach a point where they feel they have tried enough; they decide they will make do as best they can without it. In these cases, doctors might recommend another approach, such as electroconvulsive therapy.

Misdiagnosis is another factor that should be considered when many treatments fail. You may recall the category of bipolar disorder not otherwise specified, or Bipolar NOS. The patient certainly seems to have symptoms of bipolar disorder, but some of the symptoms do not fit the usual categories. For example, based on what the patient says, it is hard to tell if he has bipolar II or cyclothymia. And if a patient being treated for depression develops manic symptoms, he likely was misdiagnosed as having unipolar depression when he had a form of bipolar disorder. The doctor must be able to correctly recognize this is indeed a new development caused by the medication.

Sometimes patients will overdramatize their symptoms. Doctors are trained to recognize this, but they may not be able to do so every time. This too could lead to a misdiagnosis.

When Patients Accept Diagnosis but Resist Treatment

Another possibility is that the patient accepts a diagnosis of bipolar disorder but refuses treatment in spite of it. This problem can take three basic forms: never starting to take the prescribed medication, stopping the medication temporarily, or quitting it altogether.

Never Starting Medication

Some patients might be willing to accept that they have bipolar disorder and not get proper treatment. Generally, it is difficult to force people to take medication unless they are committed to a medical facility, are under someone's legal guardianship, or have been ordered by a court to comply with a doctor's recommendations.

In some cases, episodes of extreme moods distract patients and prevent them from thinking or caring about treatment.

In other cases, patients listen to someone other than a doctor. There might be a friend or family member who says all medications are bad or they heard of someone who had a negative experience when taking medication. An acquaintance could tell the patient that they know a religion, faith healer, or self-improvement group that can "cure" bipolar disorder. Sometimes well-meaning but misinformed people will say a cure is just a matter of more Vitamin D, a vegetarian diet, or certain exercises. If the person with a serious mood disorder trusts the third party more than his doctor, he may decide against following medical advice.

Another possibility is that the patient is afraid to go against the advice of a friend or family member. Rather than risk the anger or disapproval, he decides that living with untreated bipolar episodes is better than alienating someone he needs or trusts. This can be a problem if the patient is dependent on the third party, who consequently has a lot of influence over the patient.

Going Off Medication Temporarily

One often-discussed reason someone may temporarily go off his medication is to regain a feeling of creativity that he believes has been dampened by treatment. Some people who write, paint, compose, act, direct, sing, or dance claim they can't be creative within the less extreme range of moods re-established by treatment. Some even say they "miss" the exuberant highs that accompany mania. The fact is many people who have been successfully treated for mood disorders report that they can still do creative work when taking medication, or even do it better because they are not hampered by the self-destructive influences of out-of-control mood fluctuations. Nevertheless, a few people, to regain their lost sense of creativity, ill advisedly go off medication for a period of time when they will be performing or finishing a project. Such temporary halts in treatment can cause problems in several ways.

 ## Question

How much suffering is art worth?
Some highly regarded artists, such as Vincent Van Gogh, are alleged to have had bipolar or another mental disorder. Some people argue that the suffering such artists experienced and perhaps caused others is worth the emotional toll it took because their art enriched society as a whole. Others argue that no individual's contributions are worth disrupting a life. The answer depends on how the questioner compares the value of an individual's happiness over the value of a significant contribution to world culture.

Once off medication, for example, many of the old thoughts and behaviors associated with mental disturbance return. This can lead the patient to postpone resumption of medications until he abandons them completely. Extreme mood episodes return and the patient may pay a high price for finishing that novel or giving that concert.

With mania in particular, the patient might decide he doesn't need medication ever again. Euphoric self-confidence might lead an ill person to conclude that the only reason he was medicated was because other people were "jealous" of him. Even if someone flip-flops between taking medication and not taking medication, it is an ineffective way to treat a serious and, too often, life-threatening disorder.

Going Off Medication Permanently

Unpleasant or irritating side effects can lead people to permanently abandon medications for the same reasons that lead them to temporarily stop taking them. Frustration with medications that don't work fast enough or at all can contribute to someone deciding to stop treatment.

Other people might resent having to spend so much time getting their blood tested, answering questions, monitoring themselves, dealing with medications and doctors, and other chores that come with treating a serious mood disorder.

 Fact

An extreme example of what can go wrong when someone with bipolar disorder stops taking medications occurred in March, 2005. A twenty-eight-year-old man living in New Haven, Connecticut, had been off his medication for approximately six months when he shot at police officers three times with a sawed-off shotgun before being shot to death by officers. Before his death, he seemed hostile and short tempered, had hallucinations, and showed signs of paranoia, according to family and friends.

If you think the medical community treats you like a child or an unstable person, your pride may be wounded. Others become overwhelmed by the notion that bipolar disorder means lifelong treatment—entailing daily medication every day and routine checkups. You might decide that there has to be a better way of dealing with it. All the evidence indicates, however, that at this time there isn't a better way. Modern medicine has struggled for hundreds of years to reach the current stage of psychiatric care. It is imperfect and there is a long way to go, but as bad as some say it is, there has never been a better time in human history to receive treatment for a mental disorder.

With 15 percent or more of people with bipolar disorder dying by their own hand, and others suffering from uncontrolled manic activity, it is not easy to convince people that these reasons justify choosing florid mental illness over treatment, especially for a disorder with an 80 percent successful treatment rate.

When Patients Resist Diagnosis and Treatment

Some unfortunate individuals not only refuse treatment, but also refuse to believe they have bipolar disorder when the diagnosis is clear to others. Unless symptoms have escalated to full-scale bipolar I, it may be easy to rationalize some bipolar disorder behavior. Even people having a major manic attack may deny they are ill. Denial is one of the most daunting obstacles to treatment.

 Alert

Denial on the part of family members and loved ones is especially high during calm periods between bipolar episodes. It is then that the last episode can more easily be dismissed as an aberration, something that, although unpleasant, won't happen again. Such wishful thinking can have a negative effect on the ultimate fate of a person with bipolar disorder. Getting a professional opinion can help offset errors in self-diagnosis.

Sadly, there is still a lack of knowledge surrounding the subject of mental illness. Not realizing that bipolar and other mental disorders have a biological cause, many believe the existence of mental illness in themselves or in their family reflects badly upon them. The truth is that bipolar disorder is a disease of the brain; it is not a flaw in a person's character.

CHAPTER 9

Telling Others You Have Bipolar Disorder

Telling other people about your diagnosis can be a complicated and complex decision. Depending on your personality and situation, it may also be a straightforward exercise that requires little introspection. If and how you go about it is up to you. If you want to tell other people about your illness, how do you know whom to tell and when? How much information should you give? What if you feel uncomfortable sharing the information? Do you treat the issue differently in your personal life than your professional life? This chapter offers advice on dealing with these questions.

Why Do You Want to Tell?

Before trying to figure out what to say to someone about having bipolar disorder, figure out why you want to tell them about it. What do you hope to accomplish? You can achieve reasonable goals by sharing this information, but you should make sure you don't have unreasonable goals when you tell people about your personal medical history.

Reasonable Goals

Having reasonable goals does not mean you will achieve them—sometimes, of course, things go wrong—but it is realistic to hope that these goals might be realized:

- **Reveal the secret.** It may bother you that certain people do not know that you have bipolar disorder. You may find it a big relief to finally tell a particular person, or a group of persons, about your situation. Telling others accomplishes the goal of living without secrets if that is your choice.
- **Offer an explanation.** While there is no guarantee that others will accept what you say, you can at least try to explain some of your past behavior by talking about what it is like having a serious mood disorder. Discussing the matter openly can clear up concerns about you in the minds of others.
- **Apologize, if appropriate.** It's true you cannot help having bipolar disorder. You have not always had full control over regrettable things you've said and done. Nonetheless, when talking about your health, you might feel better if you offered an apology to certain people for past words or deeds. They may accept or reject your apology, but you have accomplished something significant if you felt the need to do it, and you did it.
- **Answer some questions.** If people have questions about what bipolar disorder is or how it relates to your situation, you can answer these questions after you tell them about your situation. Increasing understanding of mental disorders is an important contribution to promoting public education—even if done one person at a time—and reducing the stigma attached to mental illness among under- or misinformed individuals.
- **Offer other resources.** You can let people know about books or websites devoted to bipolar disorder, as well as support services for loved ones.

Unreasonable Goals

By discussing your medical history with coworkers, friends, and acquaintances, you may want to accomplish something that cannot be accomplished. Consider these warnings about unreasonable goals you might have when sharing your medical history with someone:

- **You cannot control others' reactions.** Some people might be accepting and supportive, while others might react with disbelief, anger, or shame. Some might be happy that you shared; others might cry. If you offer an apology, some people might accept it, and some might not. Some might remain an active part of your life, while others might decide to distance themselves from you. Those who remain friends may turn out to be some of your most valuable assets in life. Those who pull away were not the friends you may have thought they were. Think of the loss this way: It is good to know who is a real friend and who is not.

- **You cannot predict who will be supportive.** You might be surprised by who reacts to the news with positive support and who reacts by dismissing it. Some people may not be comfortable with the information but don't reveal their discomfort. They might try to convince you that what you've told them doesn't matter. Then they may pull away. Concentrate on the friends who stick by you.

- **You cannot control how others will use the information.** Even when sworn to secrecy, sometimes people cannot resist betraying your trust. If you confide in certain people, you should not be surprised to learn that one or more has spread the word. Also, even if you say that you do not want to be treated any differently, some people might start treating you differently, especially if they have heard about your history as gossip from someone you told.

- **You cannot predict how you will feel afterward.** In the best case, you will feel relieved after telling people about your experience with a major mood disorder. It is also possible that you will feel worried and upset; maybe it won't go as well as you hoped. Or maybe it will seem to go well, but later you'll sense discomfort in the person you told. If you are confiding in people simply to get a good feeling, you might not get it. You may feel closer to some people, but you also might feel farther from others.

Achieving Honesty

Before you tell anyone what it is like to have bipolar disorder, it is a good idea to be honest with yourself about it. You cannot expect another person to understand something if you don't understand it yourself. If this seems like a challenging task, imagine that a movie is being made about your life as a person with bipolar disorder. Think about how the story would unfold, scene by scene.

L, Essential

When explaining to someone about bipolar disorder, keep it as simple as possible. Even an attentive listener's mind may start to wander after about five minutes. Some research indicates that on average people pay attention to one out of every ten points that a speaker makes.

First, what led up to your diagnosis? What were some of the experiences or thoughts that led you to see a doctor? Did you always feel different from other people? Did you try to pretend that nothing was wrong? Did you say or do things you regretted before being diagnosed?

Second, how did you feel when you were told? Was it a relief to know that there was a name for what had been troubling you? Or were you sad to find out—or afraid, ashamed, or all three?

Third, what, if anything, is different now that you have started treatment? How do you feel about yourself now? Is the medication making a difference? What are some of the current challenges you face?

Fourth, where do you see yourself headed? Would the movie end on a hopeful note? A sad note?

Finally, in what ways are you the same person you always were? Finding out you have bipolar disorder obviously changes many things, but it does not change everything. You still probably have many of the same personal interests, likes and dislikes, and care for the same people. You are not a bipolar person; you are a human being who has bipolar disorder.

You may not have much confidence in your ability to talk about bipolar disorder, to talk about it to a particular person, or to talk about it in general if you do not feel you communicate very well. You have other options:

- **Write it down.** Some people are better at writing down their thoughts than speaking face to face. Even if it is your spouse, mother, child, or best friend, you can always write a letter to make sure you convey exactly what you want to say.
- **Seek out additional materials.** If you know of books, pamphlets, videos, or websites you think will help you say what you mean, use them. It is not cheating to rely on additional resources. Some excellent ones are available on the websites listed in Appendix B.
- **Ask loved ones to help.** If you already have one or more highly supportive people who know you have bipolar disorder, don't be afraid to ask them to help you explain it to other people who you suspect might be less supportive. It's probably a good idea to make sure that everyone already knows everyone else; it can be awkward to have strangers meeting for the first time over something so important.
- **Ask your doctor to help.** Your psychiatrist probably will not have the time to have dozens of special meetings with your loved ones. But if you would like to schedule, say, one or two special sessions in which a doctor or therapist is present to help explain what is going on, it probably can be arranged.

Telling People in Your Personal Life

Once you figure out what to say and how to say it and are clear about your goals for sharing this personal information, think about whom you want to tell. Don't automatically feel that you should tell everyone. It is perfectly normal to feel more comfortable sharing the information with some people and not others. You will probably want to start with those closest to you.

 Alert

> When you tell your children that you have a mental disorder, be careful not to turn them into your caregivers. You will remain the parent; they should still be able to be kids. You might want to talk to your doctor to discuss your specific situation before deciding how to proceed. It is also reasonable to expect there will be questions and discussions with your children over time. Make it clear that they are not to blame for your condition and that you are receiving help to keep yourself well.

Immediate Family

The information may be optional for others, but there are people in your immediate family who need to know about your diagnosis. A spouse obviously has an uncontested right to know that you have bipolar disorder. If you are dating someone and the relationship is getting serious, tell this person. It is extremely unfair to enter into a committed relationship without sharing such important information. Depending on the current state of your relationship, you might also decide to tell a former spouse, in order to make peace with your past. However, if there is a possibility that a former spouse could use this information against you, you should check with a lawyer first.

Your grown children also have a right to know you have a serious disorder that can affect personal relationships. Some would argue that you should tell them even if your relationship is strained.

There is no defined age younger children should be told. Some children are more mature than others. If you tell one of your children, but not the other, you are putting both children in an awkward position. Don't assume that children can keep secrets any better than adults.

You might want to share your diagnosis with a parent or parents. If you have difficulty communicating with a parent, you will want to take extra care when planning what to say.

Some parents blame themselves if their children have mental issues—or assume that other people will. Before telling your parents, consider how responsive they have been over the years. Have they encouraged you to seek professional help, or did they act as if nothing was wrong? Your task will be much more difficult if there has been denial in the family. If this applies to you and you feel you should tell them anyway, make it clear that your purpose is not to blame them. You also might consider getting help from your therapist or other sources before talking to them.

Do you want to tell a sibling? Some siblings are closer than others, but when it comes to something this serious, some will be supportive even if they normally are not.

Others in Your Personal Life

It is not unusual to want some friends or distant relatives to know more than you want closer relatives to know.

Depending on how close you are to them, it may be less stressful telling your grandparents, cousins, aunts, uncles, and step-relatives about being bipolar than it will telling someone in your immediate family. If you have an unusually close relationship with any of them—if a grandmother or uncle is like a parent to you—then treat that person accordingly.

Some families are larger, closer, and get together more often than others. If, for example, your parents frequently see your cousins, aunts, and uncles, it might be unrealistic to assume that this information will be kept from these other relatives indefinitely. Your parents have their own lifetime of experience with these people and may want to confide in them.

Unless you feel strongly about not wanting any of these other relatives to know about your medical history, you might want to tell them yourself. On the other hand, if you seldom see your distant relatives, it's unlikely there is a pressing need to tell them.

 Fact

Many adults are most likely to share important information with their spouses, followed by their best friends. Parents are less likely to hear such personal information from adult children, although it depends on the closeness of the relationship, of course. If, as an adult, you seldom confide in your parents, you are not alone. But if it is difficult for you to confide in your spouse, you need to seriously reconsider this most important relationship.

Since you choose your friends, they should be people you can confide in. If a so-called friend wants nothing to do with you after you tell them you are being treated for bipolar disorder, you probably have not lost much.

Besides telling friends about your diagnosis, you should also let them know how much you do or do not want to talk about it. Answer their initial questions, but if they keep bringing it up more than you want to talk about it, say so—in a nice way.

Telling People in Your Professional Life

Revealing that you have bipolar disorder may be an easy decision when it comes to close family and friends, but telling people you work with may present harder choices. This challenge is increased if your job includes being in the public eye.

Bosses and Coworkers

There are several reasons why it might be a good idea to tell people at work you have bipolar disorder. One obvious reason would be that you are close friends with someone. If a coworker or boss is someone with whom you socialize outside the office, and you have successfully confided in this person in the past, you can probably trust her. Moreover, the person might feel slighted if she ends up hearing the information from someone else.

You also might need special arrangements made for your work environment. For example, if you must take an extra-long lunch hour every Wednesday to see your doctor, you will want to inform your employer. Unless your work performance is otherwise problematic or there is a legal pre-existing policy in place given the nature of the work, it is illegal to fire you simply because you are disclosing your diagnosis.

⌐ Essential

Self-disclosure is the act of sharing something about yourself that the other person probably did not know. One of the hidden expectations of self-disclosure is that the other person will likewise share a secret about himself. This is called the norm of reciprocity.

There can be other legal considerations. You might want to consult an attorney first, but some professions might require disclosure of information such as being diagnosed with a mood disorder. If you or other people might be put at risk because, for example, one of your medications makes you drowsy, it might be best for all concerned to discuss the matter with management before something unfortunate happens. If you feel you are discriminated against after you disclose your diagnosis, you have the option of contacting an attorney, a union representative, and/or appropriate regulatory agencies to register a complaint in order to protect your rights.

You also might wish to foster a general atmosphere of trust between you and your closest coworkers. You might be lucky enough to work in a setting in which you are convinced that no one can or would use your diagnosis against you, although in a competitive working environment that is not likely to be realistic. It depends on the type of job you have and on the corporate culture or work environment in your place of employment. If you feel like you want to educate people about bipolar disorder, or it makes you comfortable sharing your story, you might have nothing to lose by doing so, but make sure you share only with people you feel you can trust.

Your Public Life

Unlike the celebrities whose photos you see on magazines at the supermarket checkout counter, your public life is separate from your professional life. But even if you are not a famous person, it is possible to go public with your experience with bipolar disorder, if you want to. For example, you could be the subject of a local news story or speak in public forums about living with a mood disorder. If you want to become an advocate for mental illness awareness by speaking to the public about your experience, anyone who meets you in the future might recognize you as someone who has a mood disorder.

This can be a useful step for you and for raising public awareness. However, you should not feel that you have to do this. Here are some questions to ask yourself if you are considering using your personal experience to raise awareness about mental disorders:

- **Are you willing to lose some privacy?** Becoming a public person might sound attractive at first, but losing even a bit of anonymity and privacy is a sacrifice you should consciously be willing to make before you get started. Before being diagnosed with bipolar disorder, did you mind much, for example, if people knew your sexual orientation or learned that you were divorced, flunked a French class, had a nose job, or any other private fact that others might prefer was kept private? If you are sensitive about being the subject of other people's conversations, going public might be more than you can handle.

- **Are you a good speaker?** Are you someone who is praised for being articulate or do you often feel you could have said something better? You do not want to say anything in public that might make you appear foolish. You also do not want to say anything that could get twisted around by a reporter or taken out of context. Previous experience with public speaking or dealing with the media is helpful. You also can improve your public speaking skills by taking classes, reading books, and practicing.

It's a good idea to learn some basic public relations skills including tips on talking to reporters, so you are sure to get your points across and not have your message misinterpreted.

- **Does your story educate, inspire, or motivate?** If so, you have a good reason for going public. You can educate people about mental illness and its treatments. You can also strive to inspire people with your story, to give hope to others who have similar challenges or who care for someone who does. A third reason is to motivate people to take action. You can promote government support for research, for example, or lobby for legislation that will benefit people struggling with mental disorders.

If your answer to all three of these questions is no, then you might want to reconsider any plans you have about becoming a spokesperson. Disclosing something personal to the general public can sometimes have a strong emotional effect on a person. Make sure you are not doing something that might make you vulnerable to either the inflated grandiosity that can come with mania or the feeling of worthlessness that can come from depression.

Fielding Questions

There are many kinds of questions you might be asked after you tell someone you have bipolar disorder. Some might be questions about the cause or nature of the disorder; others might be about you. Answer anything you feel confident answering, but remember that it's smart to say, "I don't know." Only foolish people pretend to know something when they do not.

Technical Questions

If someone asks you something about bipolar disorder and the brain, or about genetics, which is beyond your level of understanding, say so. The same holds true if you are asked, for example, how your hypomania differs from cyclothymia, and you do not honestly know the answer. Sophisticated questions about how your medication works or how it differs from other medications might likewise be answered with, "I don't know." If your manic phases rendered you unable to admit to being wrong about anything, it could be an important exercise in trust building to freely admit you don't have all the answers.

However, what you can do is suggest a source that might provide the answer. You can offer to ask your doctor the same question, but if your response to nearly every question you field is, "I don't know," it's a strong indication that you need to learn more background information about the subject.

It is important that you do not make anything up. That will hurt or destroy your credibility and potentially harm someone who needs accurate information about the nature of bipolar disorder and what it is like to live with it.

Questions about Your Past

You might be asked if something you said or did in the past was a symptom of bipolar disorder. If you have a clear sense of when you were having an episode, answer truthfully. If you are not sure, say so. People, of course, do get angry or depressed or arrogant—or make foolish, impulsive decisions—without having a bipolar episode. If a situation seems ambiguous in retrospect, it is okay not be sure why you did what you did.

⌐. Essential

The more you read, talk to experts (including your psychiatrist and therapist), and interact with other people affected by bipolar disorder, the more knowledgeable you will become. Remember, you have a background that very few doctors have: direct, first-hand experience of the disorder. Combined with textbook knowledge, your personal experience becomes a true asset when it comes to helping others understand bipolar disorder.

Honesty is the goal. After all, a main reason for discussing your experience with bipolar disorder is to help people understand you and the disorder better. There is little point in giving an answer that might be misleading just for the sake of giving an answer. Furthermore, it can help people close to you if they get accurate answers, in case they witness a future manic or depressive episode.

Questions about Your Future

You might be asked about your plans. Examples include: Will you keep working or start looking for work? What if you develop serious side effects from the medication? Will you be able to go on long vacations away from your doctor? Are you going to contact your former spouse?

You might have a sense of how you hope your future will play out. But again, if you do not know what you will be doing about something in the future, it's okay to say so. You should not make promises you cannot keep, nor should you give people false hopes. You also want to avoid creating problems by promising more than you can deliver.

Don't over commit yourself just because you're afraid of disappointing someone. Instead, try to decide with your doctor what goals are reasonable for you.

 Fact

Many people with bipolar disorder have trouble holding down a job. Research indicates that bipolar disorder makes the likelihood of employment 40 percent less likely. The good news is the odds of maintaining a job and improving work performance increase significantly with medication and therapy.

You Don't Have to Tell Everyone

There are valid reasons for wanting to share with other people the fact that you have bipolar disorder. There are also valid reasons for not sharing this information—or at least not at this time.

Is Your Medication Working?

If your medication has not yet started to work, or if you are having problems finding the right combination of medications, you might decide to wait before talking to other people about your health. Even if you feel an urge to share information about your condition immediately, weigh the pros and cons of postponing the discussion. If, for example, you think some people might worry excessively if your treatment has not yet been optimized, consider delaying the talk until you can assure them you are well on your way to controlling your mood swings.

Timing

If other major or stressful events are happening in your life, you might want to wait until things have settled down before you share the news that you have a mental disorder. Since having bipolar

disorder is big news in and of itself, planning when to tell someone is almost as important as deciding if you should tell them.
Plan it so you can explain your situation in a relaxed, stress-free
atmosphere. Doing it in the middle of a big social event such as
a wedding, funeral, birthday celebration, or business conference
probably won't give you or your listener the time and privacy the
subject requires and deserves.

Your Personal Comfort Zone

There may be plenty of people in your life who would never
know about your medical history. If, for example, you and a sibling
have never gotten along well, particularly if she lives far away, you
should not feel as though you have to tell her just because she is
your sister.

Always take your own needs into consideration. Challenge
yourself, but don't push beyond what you can comfortably handle.
If someone makes you feel unsafe or is very competitive, don't feel
obligated to tell him something so personal about yourself.

CHAPTER 10

Lifestyle Choices

Medications, such as mood stabilizers and antidepressants, are essential in the treatment of bipolar disorder. Psycho-education and therapy greatly increases the chances for keeping the disorder under control. Once extreme mood episodes are minimized, it is possible to begin making wise lifestyle choices. Successful choices can decrease the chance that a crisis will develop to trigger an episode or compel you to go off medication. Wise lifestyle choices, not so different from those made by people free of mood disorders, can have a special significance for people with bipolar disorder.

Finding the Right Job

A positive work situation makes an enormous difference in anyone's life. For a person with bipolar disorder, it can also be a way to minimize the possibility of extreme shifts of mood. If you have a mood disorder and your job involves too much stress for you to handle, consider making a change if you can.

Doing What Makes You Happy

An occupation is what you do for a living; a vocation is what you feel is your true calling in life. A few people are fortunate enough to combine the two—they pay the bills doing what they

feel they should be doing with their lives. Other people are fortunate in a different way. Their occupation is not their vocation, but
they have made peace with their situation. They are not unhappy
and they get pleasure from the things in life made possible by their
less-than-ideal job.

L. Essential

No matter how much pressure you receive or perceive from parents or
peers, you don't have to be a high-powered professional or the best
in your field. Many people have found happiness giving up presti-
gious, high-paid jobs to do something they love for much less money,
prestige, social status, and personal recognition. When you can separate what you want from what others want you to want, you will have
taken a big step toward finding a lifestyle that will make life seem
worth living.

Less fortunate people do not make peace with the knowledge
that what they do for a living is not what they want to do for a living.
Some of them become profoundly unhappy, unhappy enough at
times to become unenthusiastic and discouraged about life in general. Sometimes their unhappiness causes them to turn to alcohol
or other drugs for solace.

It is particularly important for people with bipolar disorder to
determine what makes them happy. It does not have to be what you
have always done or always assumed you would or should do. One
way to choose a first or new career is to look closely at what you
talk about with other people. Is it sports? Books? Animals? Exercise? Politics? You might be happiest if you can land a job related
to what you like to talk about, assuming it isn't malicious gossip.
Sometimes the answer is to do what has always been your most
cherished dream. But if going after that dream causes other parts
of your life to fall apart or hurts others, it might not be worth it. You
might need to find a new dream.

Avoiding Destructive Cycles

The media is full of stories about celebrities who go into rehab, only to fall back into the same destructive cycles regarding substance abuse or diet once they return to work.

 Alert

The workplace can contribute not only to stress but to early death. Men, on average, do not live as long as women. The reasons for this are not clear, although it may be because men tend to visit doctors less often than women. Men also tend to take more physically dangerous jobs than women. It's possible that men may pay a price for filling more positions, and more of the higher-status ones. The pressure of keeping these positions undoubtedly drives many men to poor health practices, stress, and early death.

Similar things happen every day to non-celebrities. Some jobs can propel some people into a cycle of negative behaviors. It might be the occupation itself or the place a person works. Here are some questions to ask about your job:

- Do you engage in substance abuse in response to upsetting things that happen at work?
- Did you start smoking after taking on this job?
- Have your eating or sleeping patterns deteriorated since starting this job?
- Do you regularly wake up in the middle of the night with anxiety related to your work?
- Are you unable to enjoy your time away from work because you cannot stop thinking about it?
- Does your job fill you with anger and rage?
- Do you find yourself wishing that bad things would happen to the people you work with?
- Does the thought of returning to work make you depressed?

- Do you have much less of a social life since taking on this job?
- During your time off, do you want to stay in bed and hide from the world, or else engage in reckless behavior such as binge spending or compulsive sex?

If you have answered yes to even one of these items, you might want to consider changing jobs. It might mean switching careers or simply finding a different position in the same field. Changing jobs takes a lot of effort, but it might be worth it if it will improve your morale and decrease your stress.

What If You Feel You Cannot Work?

Bipolar disorder may prevent you from working for short or long periods of time. Some people may not find the right combination of medications or have only partial success with their medications, and so won't be able to work full time or even part time. If you find yourself in this situation, there is no shame in admitting it. If there is a viable alternative strategy for feeding, housing, and providing basic necessities for yourself, you owe it to yourself and to others to make the choice that is best for you.

 Fact

The Job Accommodation Network provides recommendations for accommodating workers with bipolar disorder. These can include suggestions for maintaining stamina, such as flexible or part-time workloads, and ways of maintaining concentration, such as frequent small breaks, small task assignments, and a work environment with few distractions. To learn more, go to *www.jan.wvu.edu/media/Bipolar.html*.

Even if you cannot work, you can still make yourself useful in other ways, helping out around the house or doing volunteer work for a worthy cause if you are able. You can also continue to see your doctor and keep trying to find a treatment that works more effectively.

Of course, you should avoid putting yourself in a position where you are forced to live in abject poverty just to avoid job stress. Extreme poverty and homelessness are more stressful than most paying jobs. If you can find a low-paying, low-stress job that meets your basic needs—a job you can forget about when you leave—you might find it acceptable. Seek help from employment agencies and centers that provide assistance to those with mental disorders. Explain your situation, and perhaps in time you will be able to find something acceptable.

An alternative to not working at all is finding a completely different line of work. Today, most people have more than one career. You are hardly alone if you find yourself switching to a different line of work. It is also quite common for people to return to school to learn a different skill. Older returning students, or nontraditional students, are common in today's colleges and universities. If you can't afford tuition, investigate financial assistance programs, which you can find out about at a school you are interested in attending. Consider starting out in a new direction when you are ready even if you begin by taking just one class.

Essential

If you qualify, you might benefit from Social Security Disability Insurance (SSDI) or Supplemental Security Income (SSI). To find out about eligibility and how to apply, go to *www.ssa.gov*. Alternatively, you can contact your local Social Security Office listed in the phone book.

Some people cling to old habits, even bad ones, because they are familiar and seemingly less threatening than change. They tolerate dissatisfaction and unhappiness. Others claim to miss the

135

rush of adrenaline they get from working long hours to meet deadlines and competing with coworkers. For a person with bipolar disorder, such stress may increase the chances of having an extreme mood shift.

People to Avoid

Before you eventually began treatment, your actions and behavior may have alienated many people. Formerly close friends might be gone, and others, although present, might have closed themselves off from you emotionally. The same problems that drove away some people might attract less positive people. Someone who behaves erratically can attract others who behave erratically.

Those Who Interfere with Treatment

There are people who will try to discourage you from sticking to your treatment. Here is a general list of those to be wary of:

- **People with drinking or substance abuse problems who are not taking recovery measures:** Someone with several years of sobriety might make a wise and positive friend. If someone is actively abusing drugs, avoid her. A person who denies she needs help is likely to encourage you to join her and to discourage you from caring for yourself.
- **People with mood disorders who are not seeking help or taking medication:** Some mood disorders are treated with medication, some by therapy, and some by both. If it is clear that a new friend or acquaintance has bipolar or other disorder and is not getting the proper help for it, avoid him.
- **People who try to convince you to go off medication:** Whether it is because of religion, shame, or some other reason for wanting to influence your actions, anyone who tries to convince you to stop taking medication is a negative influence you don't need.

- **People with serious eating issues who are not taking recovery measures:** Someone recovering from anorexia, bulimia, or uncontrolled eating may make a good friend. But anyone actively engaging in these behaviors can encourage bad habits in you as you try to deal with bipolar disorder.

Other Negative Influences

Other people you should seriously consider avoiding are those who know little or nothing about mental disorders and have little or no empathy. Their often selfish lifestyles can lead you into behavior that could promote mood swings. Watch out for the following personal traits in the people you spend time with:

- **People who seldom sleep or slow down:** If someone is always on the go and never lets up, he is likely to be a negative influence by encouraging behaviors associated with mania.
- **People who engage in criminal activities:** Obviously, anyone would be wise to avoid involvement with a criminal, but some individuals with bipolar disorder can be taken advantage of easily. If this leads them into volatile, even dangerous, situations, the results could be tragic.
- **Thrill-seekers or people who engage in risky behavior:** People who spend a lot of money, lose a lot of money in bad investments or gambling, or put themselves in dangerous situations should likewise be avoided.
- **People who gossip excessively:** Most people gossip at times. But someone who seems to get a powerful rush by relentlessly talking about others behind their backs—most often in critical terms—takes the practice to unhealthy extremes. It's healthier not to be around them. Full-time gossips may encourage numerous traits associated with manic grandiosity.

- **People who do not like you:** It sounds obvious to avoid people who don't like us, but remarkably, it is not true for everyone. If you are desperate for friendship, you might associate with someone who likes looking down on you, pities you, or hangs out with you because no one else will hang out with her. If someone never builds you up, always criticizes or ridicules you, drop her. See a therapist. Make new friends. Just be sure to walk away from abuse and mark your action as a victory for your self-confidence and strength.

People to Seek Out

Finding good, true friends is not easy. They are rare. In fact, if you have one or two high-quality close friends you are doing very well. Most people have many acquaintances who they call friends because they interact with them in a relaxed, jovial manner. But true friends care about each other nearly as much as they care about themselves. Don't be surprised if this doesn't happen very frequently. The following people may be neutral or even positive influences in your life:

- **Other people receiving treatment for bipolar disorder:** It doesn't matter if you meet them in a support group or elsewhere, you may benefit from knowing people who have shared your experiences. You can encourage and understand each other. Also, you can offer each other helpful suggestions based on your individual experiences.
- **People getting treatment for other mood disorders or other problems:** You might be able to relate to people who are actively dealing with other types of mental or emotional issues. Again, you may be able to support and learn from each other. However, make sure that their treatment, therapy, or recovery program is real and that the person is committed to improving their health.

- **Sympathetic family members with knowledge of bipolar disorder:** When relatives understand what bipolar disorder is and is not, they can make good confidants, helpers, or assistants. Don't encourage pity. Instead, encourage constructive help and support. Be sure you don't take people's assistance for granted. It is nice if you try to return their favors, too.

⬛ Essential

The differences between men and women are always popular topics for discussion. Both sexes rate a sense of humor, intelligence, and good listening skills among the most important qualities they seek in companionship. These qualities in friends can be especially valuable if you have bipolar disorder and are trying to get your life stabilized.

There are also people who can simply be good fun to know, and whose lives are not dominated by emotional problems or dramas. If you can find people with the following traits, try to get to know them a little better:

- **People with balanced lives:** If you meet someone who takes good care of herself, eats well, gets a good night's sleep, fulfills her daily responsibilities, makes time for leisure activities, is neither a tightwad nor a spendthrift, is neither a prude nor a sex addict, and has interests in common with you, this might be a very good person to know.
- **People who treat you like an equal:** Someone who does not want to fix you, control you, or make you like him.
- **People whose company is enjoyable:** It is important for you to keep anger, gossip, and grandiosity to a minimum. If seeing someone makes you angry or feel superior, it might be best to stop socializing with her. You cannot change another person, so devote your time to people who evoke more positive feelings.

- **People who solve their problems:** Some people complain a lot, but they do not actually want anything to get better. When offered solutions to their problems, they do not act on them—they seem to prefer to be discontent rather than take steps to improve their situation. Healthy people work on fixing problems and moving on. These are people that can be fun to know because they will not overly burden you with their woes. You may also learn something from them about dealing with challenges in your own life.

Clearing Out Chaos

Coming home to clutter can put anyone into a negative frame of mind. Disorganization can promote stress and at the very least make it hard to relax. No one wants to do a task if she knows it is going to take an hour of digging through a mess just to locate what's needed to get the job done. If having a nice home sounds like an impossibly complicated task, read the following suggestions to help you get closer to achieving it.

Evaluate Your Environment

Order, rather than the scenarios described below, is obviously a better choice for someone with bipolar disorder. If any of the following scenarios sound familiar, you probably will benefit from a bit more organization.

- Before leaving for work, you frantically rush around at the last minute looking for your car keys. Your day gets off to a hyper, distracted start. You have a constant feeling of unease because you frequently can't locate things.
- After a hard day at work, you come home to the same depressing mess. Without consciously realizing it, it can reinforce the notion that your life is a depressing affair or that life itself is chaotic and ugly.

- A common task no one enjoys, such as paying bills, can take twice as long. You have to clear off space and find what you need to complete the routine chore. This makes the task even more unpleasant. You might put it off until the last minute and then become stressed as you scramble to get it done against a deadline.
- You are too embarrassed to have people come to your home because it looks so bad, or people do not like visiting you for the same reason. This keeps you separated and disconnected from other people. It can also reinforce a sense of inadequacy—"normal" people can have houseguests, but not you.
- Living in a mess reinforces notions of unworthiness and keeps you from feeling relaxed even in your own home. This may cause you to treat yourself less often to quiet, relaxing times.
- Because it is so unpleasant to be home, you become overly restless and impatient to get out of the house. You stay out later than you should, spend too much money, and associate with the wrong people, just to avoid being home.

What Is an Orderly Home?

Here are ways to increase order in your refuge from the outside world. In contrast to the chaos described previously, consider the following scenarios:

- You open your eyes in the morning to pleasant surroundings. You do not fret about your car keys because you have a place to keep them. You leave for work after a nice breakfast, feeling energized to face your day.
- You enjoy coming home from work because you like your home. You may or may not have much money, but there are at least a few objects in your home that make you feel content or inspired.

- It is time to pay the monthly bills, so you turn on your favorite music and go to the drawer where you keep your checkbook, calculator, stamps, and envelopes. (Or, if you pay your bills online or have an online bill-paying service, you check the numbers.) A screw on a kitchen drawer needs tightening, but it only takes a moment to get the screwdriver out of the toolbox and fix it. The rest of the evening is yours to enjoy.

- You look forward to having friends visit. People often comment that they enjoy your home. You visit their homes in return, and have active, normal friendships.

- After a trying day at work, you can relax at home. It is a place away from outside stresses where you can watch a movie, read a book, work on a hobby, or listen to music.

 Fact

According to many surveys, vision is the most important sense for most people. We visually take in much more information than we hear, taste, smell, or touch. Visually pleasant versus unpleasant surroundings can have a major impact on how we view our lives and ourselves. This is true for people with and without mood disorders, but because people with bipolar disorder are often more sensitive to stresses, they may benefit from a visually pleasant environment even more.

The inscription over the temple of Apollo at Delphi in ancient Greece translates as: Know Yourself; Nothing in Excess. This advice applies to setting your personal priorities as well as organizing your home. Strive for relaxed order in both; neither excessive activity nor obsessive order is healthy. Try to keep yourself and your home relaxed, efficient, and in tune with your interests and needs.

Replace Fanaticism with Tranquility

Some people become so fanatical about neatness that they make life hell for others—or themselves. It is as if a home is not for living in, just to be admired. These people often have domineering personalities, yet underneath they may have little confidence and a weak self-image because they live to impress others. This type of fanaticism can suggest manic-like symptoms. It can also swing to depression when the slightest thing in the house seems to be amiss.

Are You a Fanatic Around the House?

Ask yourself the following questions to get an idea of whether or not you're a fanatic around the house:

- Do you spend all your money, bounce checks, or run up huge credit card bills in order to buy things for your home?
- Are you sometimes late for appointments or do you miss activities because you "must" clean around the house?
- Do you get more angry than necessary when someone disturbs something in your home?
- Are even the little things you do for yourself overly regimented? For example, do you decide you must take your evening bath at 7:30 P.M. and become extremely upset when a phone call compels you to take it at 8:00?
- Have people ever inquired as to whether you might be obsessive-compulsive?

If you answered yes to any of these questions, you might benefit by discussing it with a therapist or doctor.

Ask for Help

A great way to be both relaxed and organized is to seek help from others. If you do not have much money, you can turn to the people you know to help you reduce costs. For example, you can invite people over to a painting party. Or simply ask family and friends to help you organize your place or go shopping with you—being careful, of course, not to overspend. Some people enjoy helping with these kinds of tasks, so do not be shy about asking if you think you are asking sympathetic people. If you get a poor response or turnout, make another plan or do the job yourself.

If you can afford it, consider hiring professionals to repair your home or apartment, organize it, and redesign it. Professional organizers can help you get control of clutter and prioritize your time. They can arrange to design, build, or buy shelves, closet organizers, file cabinets, or drawers if you need them to get and stay organized. Good advisors will work with you to develop easy ways of keeping things orderly. They specialize in helping people; you should not feel embarrassed by what you need help with or by the fact that you don't know how to do it yourself. If you can't afford it, there are many do-it-yourself books on the subject in libraries.

Essential

If you have poor housekeeping skills, or just hate housework, consider hiring a housekeeping service. You might hire someone to come in once a week—or even once a month—to thoroughly clean your place. If you cannot afford to pay someone, consider bartering or trading favors with a neighbor or friend.

Through banks and online services, you can arrange to have your monthly bills paid automatically each month. If you simply do not trust online services—or computers—you might be able to hire an accountant to take care of your monthly expenses. You should ask for references, to make sure it is a reputable and honest service. (As a precaution, sign all the checks yourself once your accountant has prepared them.) And if you cannot afford an accountant, you might barter services with a qualified friend or relative.

CHAPTER 11

Developing a
Good Self-Image

Other steps you can take to bring more stability into your life concentrate on developing your inner strengths. They involve introspection, examination of your strengths and weaknesses, and gaining a good understanding about the ways you relate to other people and what to expect—or not expect—from them.

Dealing with the Past

When you start to regain control of your moods after you begin treatment, you look back on the impressions you made on people in the past. You probably said or did some troubling or unpleasant things that were beyond your control. Your past, therefore, may have a significant impact on how people relate to the news that you have a mood disorder.

Some People May Be Relieved

Some people who have known you for a while probably figured out that you were ill. They may even have picked bipolar disorder as the most likely reason for your behavior. Some may have encouraged you to seek professional help. These are the people that are most likely to tell you they are relieved that you finally got help, and that your problem turned out to have a name. There is a good chance they will be supportive.

Other people, by contrast, might have distanced themselves from you for their own safety, comfort, or other reasons. It is important that you respect these decisions. Over time you may be able to build or rebuild a closer relationship with them as you get control of your moods. It is always important, of course, that you respect other people's needs. With effective treatment, you should be able to do this, especially if you are willing to change your old behavioral patterns.

Some People May Refuse to Accept It

There may be people in your past who tried to ignore or dismiss your erratic tendencies. They may even have convinced themselves that you were not ill. Perhaps treating mental illness with medication is against their religion. Perhaps they don't trust or believe in psychiatry. They might think it weak or indulgent to accept a diagnosis of mental disorder.

Whatever the reason, these people may persist in their denial and perhaps respond with a bit of anger or irritation. It would not be surprising if, underneath their denial or anger, they are not completely surprised by your diagnosis. Over time, they might concede that maybe your doctor was right after all. In the meantime, try to remember that their reaction is not about you; it is more likely about their inability to face the reality of mental illness.

Some People May Feel It's Too Little Too Late

If, in the throes of mania or depression, you said or did things that hurt or frightened others, they might be unwilling to give you a chance to make amends. You might have wounded them too deeply for them to want you in their lives even after your treatment begins to stabilize your moods.

If you feel it is important to explain yourself or apologize, then do it for yourself. Don't expect them to forgive you completely. It may do more harm than good if you minimize what you did; be honest with yourself and with them. It's true, you may not have been able to control your behavior at the time, and you will gain nothing by blaming yourself. Remember that another person's sense of well-being is not a trivial matter.

Everyone has the right to set her own boundaries. Especially if you are divorced or estranged from someone, you should not try to push your way back into his life after you begin treatment.

Some people may thank you for taking responsibility and expressing regret for your actions, and then make it clear, verbally or nonverbally, that they don't want to resume a friendship with you. Others might respond with anger, and feel you are just trying to make excuses for yourself. Don't argue—you can apologize and excuse yourself or politely leave after letting the person vent a little while.

Dealing with Family Shame

Despite all that is known about mental illness, there are still people who think it amounts to a curse or is a sign of personal weakness. Upon hearing that a loved one has bipolar disorder, these people might misguidedly decide that the most important thing is protecting the family reputation. Rather than making sure you get help, they might even try to dissuade you from doing anything about it. Even if they support treatment, they might be horrified to learn that you have told people outside the family.

Religion

Some families belong to religious groups that disapprove of treating ill people with medication. According to these groups, practicing the principles of the religion is the only way to fight disease.

Parents who belong to these groups have denied their children standard, proven medical treatments. Adult family members are technically free to make their own choices regarding their use of modern medicine, but they may decide not to get treatment either because of their beliefs or because they don't want to present the family in a negative light in the eyes of their fellow religionists. The results of such decisions can be tragic.

If you have bipolar disorder and religion is important to you, you might try to find a group that meets your spiritual needs but does not make blanket judgments about all modern medical treatment. Many religions have an alternate view that humankind should use its knowledge to help and to heal. For these religions, using the advances of modern medicine, including psychiatry, does not interfere with their belief in God or in religious teachings.

Status or Class

Rich or poor, many families are extremely concerned about what other people think of them. They worry that if everything does not appear perfect, others will judge them as unworthy. There is nothing wrong with wanting your loved ones to be successful, but linking your self-worth to the material and social success of your children or siblings can create problems when expectations are not realized. In such a family, it is possible that someone that has bipolar disorder will be seen as lowering the family's status or class—as if only inferior families are affected by mental disorders.

 Fact

Notorious spree killer Charles Starkweather was executed at age nineteen in 1959. At one point, his attorneys urged him to plead insanity in order to spare his life. Starkweather's mother told him to go to the electric chair instead, because it would shame the family to have someone labeled mentally unfit.

It might be helpful to point out the famous, distinguished people who have been diagnosed with mood disorders and how bipolar disorder has often been associated with creativity. You also might teach your family that bipolar disorder is an illness with a biological basis. Thinking of mental illness in terms of social status, success versus failure, or respectability versus shame amounts to denying centuries of progress in our understanding of brain disorders.

The public often admires individuals who courageously step forward and admit to human imperfections. Former First Lady Betty Ford became even more admired when she publicly discussed her problems with alcohol and substance abuse. Many other celebrities have evoked outpourings of public support after they have gone public with their struggles with psychiatric issues.

Getting Your Priorities in Order

Having a sense of purpose in life means having a clear idea of what your priorities are—what really matters and what doesn't. If your moods are not stable, it will affect all aspects of your life. It may not be obvious today, but tomorrow or in two weeks, things that seem to be going right might start to go terribly wrong.

 Question

Where can you learn about new therapies and medications?
At least two frequently updated websites can help you find potential new treatments for bipolar disorder and other medical conditions. The U.S. National Institutes of Health (*www.clinicaltrials.gov*) allows you to locate clinical trials by medical condition, location, or sponsor. This site also includes useful background information and a definition of terms related to new drug trials. CenterWatch's (*www.centerwatch .com*) website can also help match patients with new clinical trials.

If your treatment is working, stick with it. The odds are that you are one of the 80 percent of patients who eventually settle on a treatment plan that eliminates or greatly reduces the number and severity of future episodes. Even if everything else goes wrong on a given day, you have done the most important thing if you took your medication. Give yourself great credit for that accomplishment, which many others cannot manage to do. It will at least enable you to face setbacks with the same emotional resources most resilient people can rely on when dealing with routine problems.

If you are still looking for the right treatment, don't give up. Unless multiple doctors agree that the possibilities have been exhausted, keep trying different combinations. If you hear of a new medication, ask your doctor about it.

If you cannot take medication, try different approaches until something becomes available. Get as much information as you can from your doctor or other reliable sources about ways to reduce stress and other triggers that lead to mood swings. Don't drink or use illegal drugs. Keep your eyes and ears open to alternative treatments, seek out therapists and support groups, and also keep in mind the possibility of newer medications that might work for you.

(Self-)Honesty Is the Best Policy

How do you know if you are doing a better job of running your life? How do you know if you are genuinely connecting to other people in a positive way? There are a number of steps you can take to find answers to these questions. It is important as you evaluate your progress that you not be overly critical but still truthful with yourself.

Develop a Checklist

Decide what sorts of things you want to accomplish in a given day, week, month, year, or five years. Check off these long-term goals, such as going back to school or starting to learn a new trade, once you have accomplished it. They can also be ongoing goals that you can check off every day such as:

- I'm eating and sleeping regularly.
- I'm finishing one task before starting another one.

- I seek help from friends or a therapist when I start to feel stressed or overwhelmed.
- I get help when I want to abuse alcohol and other drugs.

You share one significant similarity with other people who have bipolar disorder—your diagnosis—but you remain an individual. Your checklist may include many of the same items found on the lists of others, but it also may include items unique to you. Consider getting some input or suggestions from your doctor or therapist. The purpose of this list is to figure out how mania and depression each tend to steer your life off course, and what sorts of things you can do each day to ward off episodes.

If you are doing these things each day—whether they are specific actions or changes of attitude—you are on the right track. But an outstanding checklist means nothing if you are not using it honestly to keep track of your progress. At the same time, you do not need to be your harshest critic. Never put yourself down; sadly, there never seems to be a shortage of other people who will do that for you. It is your job to build yourself up and associate with people who will honestly help you do that. If you slip, don't obsess with guilt. Instead, think in terms of "needs improvement," or "needs more work." It is part of the process.

Therapy

It is normal to change your mind, to go from happy to sad, or to reinterpret a situation. It is even normal to wonder sometimes about who you are or what you want. But untreated bipolar disorder causes such extreme fluctuations that the task of gaining self-knowledge can become impossible.

A good therapist can help you get a clear idea of what you need to be content and satisfied in life, what your strengths and weaknesses are, and how you perceive yourself.

When you feel uncertain and confused, tell your therapist. Such troubling feelings could actually be a good development, a positive phase in your recovery as you let go of some of your old assumptions. It also might indicate that a particular therapy is simply not working, and that this is not the right therapist for you. If you have given a therapist weeks or months of honesty during your sessions and you still don't feel comfortable with her, try another one.

 Fact

Social learning theory posits that we learn how to behave by imitating others. For example, children will learn to be abusive or kind by watching how adults around them behave. This process of basing your behavior on what you see others do is called modeling.

Honesty with Others

Knowing how to say things that are accurate and in just the right way is a learned skill, a balancing act that will sometimes fail, no matter who you are and what your background is.

Possibly the question people ask each other most often is, "How are you?" The common response is, "Fine." It is polite small talk.

 Alert

Many people do not realize that self-disclosure is a selective process. No one ever tells another person *everything* about himself; even the closest of relationships involve some secrecy. Just because someone tells you one of his secrets, it does not mean he has told you everything about himself.

For someone with a mood disorder, however, "How are you?" can be a very important question, much more than small talk. There is nothing harmful in polite small talk, but you should have people in your life you can answer honestly, "I'm not fine." When depression strikes, it is essential that you connect with someone, a friend or family member, and see your psychiatrist and perhaps your therapist.

On the other hand, if you are teetering on a manic episode, you might be unable to stop talking. It helps if other people in your life know the warning signs and can encourage you to get professional help. It is crucial that your doctor is aware of extreme mood changes. You may need different medications and ways to help change your exposure and/or reaction to things in your life that promote episodes.

Learning to Problem Solve

You will find it useful to approach problems logically, and with a certain amount of detachment. Many people struggle to accomplish this. If you can develop skills in this area, problems may not be as stressful as they would be otherwise. Some can even change from being problems into interesting challenges.

Break Down the Problem

Let's say you don't have transportation: no car, no bus service, and no budgeted money for a taxi. You need to get to the drugstore across town to pick up a prescription. A friend agreed to get it for you, but then your friend leaves a message saying she cannot run the errand, after all. There is no one else who lives in town that you feel comfortable calling.

You can get upset because the problem seems impossible to solve and you are scared of what might happen if you do not get your medication in time, or you can break down the problem into a series of steps:

1. Are you sure there is no one else, such as a neighbor, you can call to run the errand as a favor?
2. Can you offer to pay someone a few dollars for his time, or if you are broke, to give him an IOU to dinner or a movie? Can you offer to work for him to repay him?

3. Can you shift your budget to find the money for a cab? Can you give up the dinner out or the movie you were planning? If you think it will be too expensive, is there something else you can do without? Can you borrow from next month's budget, giving you more time to find a solution and replace the self-loan?

4. If there is no cab, how far is it to walk safely? Would walking for, say, an hour or so this one time really be out of the question if you could do it safely?

5. Could you call your doctor's or therapist's office and ask them for suggestions? Perhaps they could send the prescription to a pharmacy closer to you.

6. To avoid this situation in the future, are you sure there are no social services or charities available that could provide transportation or run the errand for you once a month? Check with your public library, social services department, city hall, or place of worship to find out.

Rather than letting yourself feel hopeless and upset, it is possible to think logically about what to do, step by step. With analysis, the problem may not be more than you can handle.

Produce More Than One Solution

Critical thinking is the ability to look at a situation from more than one point of view. Answers to problems don't usually appear by themselves; they are developed and implemented as a result of effort. It is usually a mistake to think in terms of finding the one ultimate solution. Both for your peace of mind and for practical considerations, it is a good idea to always have a Plan B—or even a Plan C.

For instance, using the example described above: If you call for a cab, make sure you leave enough time to get there some other way, even if it means walking. If it turns out there is a special shuttle service for people with disabilities, by all means arrange to use it.

But maybe you can also call your friend back and say, "I have made arrangements so that I will not have to take advantage of your generosity anymore. But just in case the shuttle can't make it one day, is it still okay if I ask for your help?" (And show your appreciation to your friend. It will make you feel better about taking her help and it may make her feel good knowing you appreciate her efforts.)

Rather than frantically trying to convince yourself that you should not be worried about things going wrong, take that nervous energy and put it to good use by developing an alternative plan that will decrease your anxiety. Turn your worry into planning.

Remember the Big Picture

Losing a sense of perspective can inspire dramatic shifts of mood for people with bipolar disorder.

It is a good idea to keep the problems of everyday life in perspective. Again, using the same example: Was it that big a deal that you were inconvenienced for an afternoon or so in order to get your medication? Comparing the positive aspects and potential of your life to the disadvantages and misfortunes common in the world may help you maintain a sense of perspective. What if you were living in a time or place where your medication did not exist? What if you were one of those less fortunate people who do not respond to medication? What if other health concerns incapacitated you? By comparison, you may be better off than many other less fortunate people living today in parts of the world that see unending war and oppression. There are many things worse than being medicated for a treatable illness like bipolar disorder.

Additionally, it might help if you asked yourself if there are other things you did recently that went according to plan, which made you feel good. Is there a recent or past large or small success that might help offset the setback? What are your long-range goals, and in general are you making progress toward achieving them? This type of questioning can help you maintain perspective.

CHAPTER 12

Managing Mania

Even if someone responds well to mood stabilizers, it's possible at times she will find herself edging toward hypomania or even full-scale mania. A relapse might be traced to a specific event or might appear without an obvious trigger. It's also possible that the prescribed mood stabilizer is not 100 percent effective. In any case, there are things a person can do to maintain an even pace of life, reduce stress, and, according to many patients and doctors, reduce the chances of a relapse and hospitalization.

Be Prepared

No matter how long it has been since you had a hypomanic or manic episode, there is always a possibility you will have another one. Of course, feeling a bit on edge or having to stay up late to finish a project doesn't necessarily mean you are on the verge of becoming manic. You can protect yourself from real crises by realizing that certain situations might increase the likelihood of mania. Recognizing specific triggering events or patterns of behavior that are especially relevant to your particular illness can save you, and those around you, a lot of pain and inconvenience.

Stay Out of the Fast Lane

From time to time, everyone is rushed—especially with instant communication technology like mobile phones, handheld computers, and instant messages delivered over wireless Internet networks. Many people cannot avoid having to do several things at once, as quickly as possible. You have to hurry to a store before it closes, but only after you get to a gas station to fill the tank. Your boss wants a report finished by noon, but you have other deadlines the same day. Or you are cooking Thanksgiving dinner for your entire family, an exercise that often requires dealing with various personalities and a full to-do list of shopping and kitchen chores. Despite these sometimes unavoidable challenges, there are some things you can do to achieve a life less likely to be interrupted by manic episodes:

- Try to avoid highly stressful jobs. For example, if a job involves a lot of last-minute deadlines or waiting on many customers who all want service immediately, it might not be right for you. Even if the job seems relatively low key, it can be made stressful by a less-than-enlightened boss or fellow employee who makes the work environment unpleasant. If you find yourself in an environment that overly stresses you, seek a better job. You may not find it, but the benefits are worth the effort no matter how long the search takes.

- If you are lucky enough to find one, a job that gives you some freedom to pace yourself, provides flexibility, offers frequent short breaks, and either is staffed by understanding people or gives you a degree of autonomy might be better for you. While many people would love to have such a job, remember that if you have a disability due to bipolar disorder, you may be entitled to certain on-the-job considerations thanks to the Americans with Disabilities Act. To determine if you qualify, visit the website (*http://askjan.org/corner/vol02iss04.htm*).

- Obviously, try to avoid highly stressful situations. Plan your day carefully to avoid unnecessary rushing. You may not have to perform some tasks, errands, or favors that someone else can do or that don't need to get done. Don't make unnecessary work and stress for yourself.
- Ask for help when appropriate. If you volunteer to cook Thanksgiving dinner or take on some difficult task at work, ask for help. If you can turn something into a team effort, it may be less stressful if your responsibility is clearly defined and you don't assume total responsibility.
- Pace yourself. Take short breaks whenever possible. Step outside and get some fresh air. Have a snack. Read a few more pages of a book, listen to some music, or take some deep breaths. Pause at times to look around you. You do not need to compete with everyone. Remember that the task you are performing may be important, but with perspective, it may not be worth the worry it causes you. Strive to keep events in perspective.
- Avoid putting things off until the last minute. If you can do part of a task on one day and a little more the next, you can avoid rushing around at the last minute to meet a deadline. This can decrease stress.

 Fact

Stress has been estimated to cost the U.S. workplace around $300 billion each year. This figure includes compensation claims related to stress, health insurance and medical costs, absenteeism, employee turnover, and reduced productivity. Upward of 40 percent of the workers who experience job burnout claim that stress is the main problem.

Pay Attention to the Calendar

Some dates might be associated with a manic episode. These can include the following:

- **Cycles:** Be aware of the patterns if your history of manic or depressive episodes tends to run in cycles. For example, if mania typically followed depression, you should be prepared for the possibility that you are vulnerable to mania or hypomania if you have recently been feeling down.
- **Seasons:** Seasonal changes are sometimes associated with dramatic mood swings in some people with mood disorders. Be especially careful to avoid high-energy behavior during such times.
- **Anniversaries:** The anniversary of a major life event can potentially trigger a manic episode. This is especially likely when the event is associated with a loss of some kind such as divorce, the death of a loved one, or other troubling event, including a major mood episode. In all of these instances, memories of the emotions felt at the time—even ones you might not be consciously aware of—can contribute to an episode.
- **Forthcoming events:** Whether it is something stressful (such as a court date) or something potentially positive (such as a marriage or promotion at work), a major change can set in motion a manic episode. It is a good idea to discuss in advance with your doctor or therapist how to deal with significant forthcoming events that will have a big impact on your life.

Essential

Contacting your doctor when you recognize thoughts, feelings, or behaviors that precede a manic episode can be one of the best ways to head off a developing problem. She can provide temporary, supplemental medications and monitor you to help stabilize your mood, prevent a major disruptive mood swing, and keep you out of the hospital.

Warning Signals

Become familiar with the warning signs that seem to apply especially to you. They could help you avoid a manic episode. They may be found in your thinking patterns, feelings, and changes in the way you act. Make a list of changes that you suspect precede your episodes. Learn to spot them early. Respond right away by slowing down and getting help from your doctor or therapist. Here are some of the areas in which you can monitor yourself for marked changes indicating a potential manic episode:

- **Speech patterns:** Are you talking more rapidly than normal? Are you having trouble not talking? Is your voice louder than usual? Are you getting hoarse more often? If you are not face to face with others, do you feel compelled to write a letter, send an e-mail, or talk on the phone so you can keep communicating nonstop?
- **Eating and sleeping:** Are your eating and/or sleeping patterns dramatically changing?
- **Busy without productivity:** Are you always active, yet accomplishing little? Do some of the tasks you take on have no purpose?
- **Irritability:** Are you more easily irritated than usual? Do small things annoy you more than usual?
- **Feeling threatened:** If you do not get your own way or are interrupted, do you feel much more threatened and hostile than usual? Do you find yourself wanting to argue with people more than usual?
- **Lavishness:** Are you suddenly spending more money, giving more gifts, and/or taking more trips? Are you suddenly living beyond your means?
- **Interference:** Are you suddenly giving people advice whether they want it or not? Do you feel like you are being exceptionally generous as you do so, as though

you are a superior person bestowing wisdom upon a lesser being?
- **Behavior with strangers:** Are you suddenly overly friendly, generous, or nosy toward people you have never met? Are you asking inappropriate questions of strangers or engaging in high-risk behavior with them including sex?
- **Heightened drama:** In general, are you feeling a need to stand out from the crowd—to talk, act, or dress differently—in a way that makes everyone notice you? Whether angry or happy, is the feeling suddenly more intense, as though you'll never stop being angry or never stop laughing?

The general impressions of other people—coworkers, acquaintances, friends, or family—can give you a hint that something might be happening to you that may require medical attention. People who care about you and are familiar with your diagnosis might tell you that you seem to be edging toward an episode. They might put it in the form of a question, such as, "Are you feeling okay?" "Do you think you are having a problem?" or "Have you talked to your doctor about the way you're acting?" Or they might simply comment that you seem much more agitated and perhaps you should get some extra help. If you pay attention to these warnings and get a doctor's opinion, you might be able to prevent a disruptive episode.

People you know—but who do not know you have bipolar disorder—also might notice that something seems wrong. They may observe, "You seem on edge lately" or ask you if "something happened that I don't know about, because all of a sudden you have a very short fuse." They also might express naïve puzzlement over something you did, such as how you were able to afford something you purchased. They might wonder when you started picking up strangers in bars or remark that they never knew you were such an angry or funny person. People you work with might wonder aloud why you did not finish your work as you normally do or that you must have stayed up all night getting something done in record time.

Such hints, clues, and warnings can alert you to the possibility that your mood is changing in a negative way. If you make yourself sensitive to them, you increase your chances of averting an episode by taking action and getting help.

 Fact

> People you don't know well can also give you valuable input if you learn to pay attention to their reactions to you. If you go too far with strangers, they might tell you to go away, stop asking them questions, stop trying to buy them drinks, etc. If the encounter escalates to shouting, or even violence, it has reached the stage beyond a warning. Get help right away. At the other extreme, a stranger might tell you that you are the friendliest or funniest or smartest person they ever met. Use these clues to evaluate your condition and seek help if you need it.

Protect Your Personal Life

Before you have a relapse, there are precautionary steps you can take to keep your personal life intact. Ideally, you will get help before things digress too far. You can try to minimize the negative consequences for you and those you care about if you should have a manic episode by following some of these suggestions.

Preparing Your Loved Ones

The people closest to you—your spouse, children, other family members, and close friends—should be aware of your illness and should know its implications. Tell them what it's like to have the disorder and how it affects you. Give them a list of warning signs and ask for their help in keeping an eye on your behavior. Give them a list of outside resources, including contact information for your doctor(s), therapists, support groups, and others who might help if you need it.

The Aftermath

After a minor or major relapse, talk to everyone who might have been affected by it. Group counseling could help if the episode caused significant problems for people affected by it. Your therapist might be able to guide you in how best to communicate with different people.

If you had a manic episode because you deliberately chose to go off your medication, you may owe some people an explanation and/or an apology. If the episode was unavoidable and happened despite your best intentions and efforts, you may still want to discuss how the experience affected you and encourage those affected by it to discuss its affects on them.

 Alert

> Here are some good ways to respond when you feel a mania or hypomania episode coming on. Contact your doctor or therapist. Consciously strive to calm down—mentally, emotionally, and physically. Take time off from work if possible. Avoid stimulation and people who seek it. Retreat to a place free of distractions where you can practice calming activities such as yoga, meditation, or a hobby. Strive to replace negative thoughts with neutral or positive thoughts.

Don't assume you know how another person feels or what it was like dealing with you when you were in a manic state. Ask them, and let them tell you what it felt like for them. Avoid responding defensively, correcting their experiences, or keeping the focus solely on you. This is where a professional therapist or counselor can help by moderating the discussion and keeping it on track for the benefit of everyone participating.

What if You Have Done Things You Regret?

In the best of circumstances, you did not do anything so damaging it cannot be undone. Without trivializing the feelings of a loved one who has been insulted, embarrassed, humiliated, or feared for their own safety or yours, if you did not complete a life-changing act such as having an affair, leaving your spouse, depleting family savings, quitting your job, selling the house, or disowning a child, you and those affected should be able to recover with time and effort.

 Fact

> Some ways of responding to a developing manic mood can make things worse. Ignoring the signs, avoiding your doctor, turning to alcohol, going shopping, and trying to distract yourself by doing something stimulating can have disastrous consequences.

If, however, you did do something drastic, you need to realize that those you hurt may not be able to let you back into their lives—or at least not for a while. Because dramatic changes work against mood stabilization, it is likely you will need help dealing with this consequence of your relapse. If, for example, your spouse has decided to leave you—or you left him or her while you were manic—you might need to accept this change as best you can, with your doctor's help.

If, despite your actions, your inner circle remains essentially intact—for example, your spouse wants you back—it is time to think seriously about what you can do to prevent or at least limit the damage that might result from another major episode. Talk to your doctor about it. If it appears there is little you can do to prevent future episodes, you and your spouse need to reach an understanding about how to proceed—preferably with the guidance of a doctor or therapist.

Protect Your Assets

There are steps you can take to try to minimize damage to your finances, property, or other assets should you have a manic episode.

Ironically, the more you have, the more you can do to protect yourself; the less you have, the more you can lose. But whether rich or poor, you might find some of the following suggestions useful.

Pay for Safety

If you are moderately well off, you might find it worthwhile to make a few expenditures as insurance against losing virtually everything. For instance, consult with an attorney about matters such as requiring the co-signature of a spouse—or even a neutral third party—before you can spend, sell, trade, or give away money or assets that exceed a predetermined amount. Such consultations might also involve an accountant, banker, or stockbroker.

Also, you can set up a system that provides you with an allowance. With an attorney and accountant, you can agree to have access to a predetermined amount of cash per week. You could arrange this so you have access to a certain amount per month or year, but smaller amounts accessed over shorter time periods will probably lessen the possibility of large-scale irresponsible spending. Finally, consider creating an advance directive.

Advance Directives

An advance directive is a legal document. It gives permission for another individual, such as a doctor or family member, to make medical decisions and ensure proper treatment—even hospitalization—in the event the signer has a relapse. Some states allow a person who is free of symptoms to sign such a document, spelling out how he wants to be treated if symptoms pose a threat to his well-being. For instance, it is possible to define the kind of assisted treatment to be provided, who should provide it, and who should be responsible for the patient. Check with your psychiatrist, other mental health care providers, and a lawyer to find out if your state allows such contracts and if one would be right for you.

Limit Your Liquid Assets

If most of your finances are tied up in investments that you cannot access without third-party intervention, there are fewer liquid assets for you to waste in a frenzy of mania. If you must use a credit card, make sure it has a low cash limit. Although it can have your name on it, make sure someone else must agree before the limit can be increased.

If you have a checking account, make it a joint account with a trusted party who has power of attorney. That way, if you seem to be out of control, your checking account partner can close the account. You can also set up the account to require joint signatures on all checks. Although this can be inconvenient, it can prevent a lot of trouble if you are prone to manic episodes despite treatment. At many banks, you can set up a checking account to provide coverage in case of overdrafts. This isn't a good idea if you are likely to go on spending sprees during a manic episode. If you have overdraft protections, make sure it is limited.

In addition to a lawyer, you can talk to your banker about other steps you can take to limit your liquid assets. You don't need to share everything about why you want certain precautionary measures in place; the main point is that you want to prevent overspending.

What if You Do Not Have Much to Start With?

Millions of people in the United States now live one or two paychecks away from poverty—they have no savings, property, or valuable heirlooms. If you are one of these people, you can't afford lengthy consultations with attorneys or accountants, and you may not have a bank account.

There are, however, inexpensive or even free legal services in many communities. If you are a college student, there might be a legal aid service provided by your school or at a law school nearby. Law libraries provide examples of different kinds of legal documents. You can also consult online links for such examples, including *http://ppc.uslegalforms.com* and *www.legalzoom.com*. While an attorney should still look these over, you can do at least some of the work yourself.

You can avoid having access to multiple credit cards, and you can place a limit on the credit they provide. Also, you can have some safety precautions in place on any bank account you do have. Enlist the aid of a counselor, therapist, or other advisor you trust to help you take advantage of these strategies to protect yourself.

If you bounce checks as the result of a manic episode, you will face high overdraft charges. Again, you might consider setting up a checking account that requires someone to co-sign your checks. You also might severely limit your access to checks and credit cards, dealing mainly with budgeted cash where possible. You can still use a bank check or a money order when paying rent or other important bills so you have proof you paid.

Protect Your Professional Life

If you have a job, you do not want to jeopardize it or cause problems for your coworkers or clients if you have a manic or hypomanic episode. There are some steps you can take to try to protect your position or your career.

Allow for Missing Work

If you feel you are sliding into a manic or hypomanic state, consider taking time off from work in the form of sick days or vacation until your mood can be stabilized. Your employer should be aware of your condition if you need time off because of it. If you hold a position of great responsibility and have made yourself indispensible to your employer, it is a good idea to develop plans and procedures so other employees can take over in your absence. It is nice to be considered important, but if your symptoms are not under control you might want to avoid the pressure of being indispensable.

Some people have jobs from which it is difficult or impossible to take time off. They may not be paid if they don't show up or the boss may pressure or threaten workers who need time away from the job. If your supervisor fires people who take time off for illness or legitimate reasons, you will be helping yourself if you mount a serious search for another job. You need to have some flexibility if you are subject to relapses for bipolar disorder.

Self-employed individuals should live within a budget so they have backup funds when work is slow. If you are self-employed and have bipolar disorder with relapses, this advice is especially important. Ideally, you should have enough assets to cover your expenses for a few days or a week off now and then to attend to your mental health. If you are in business with someone else, ask that person to fill in for you and make it up to her with money or by covering for her at another time.

If Work Cannot Be Avoided

If people are depending on you to finish or do something by a certain date or if not doing it for any reason would end your career, you should talk to your doctor about what steps you can take to minimize the onslaught of mania. Even here, your mental health should come first. But there are some things you can do in the meantime:

- Pace yourself as best you can. Whatever the pressure, you can still take short breaks to get at least a few minutes of fresh air, and remember to eat and sleep.
- Take steps to counter the high energy. When you are done working at the end of the day, take a long hot bath, meditate, listen to calming music, read or watch TV, or do whatever you need to do to calm down.
- Stay in close touch with your doctor or other sources of support. Let him know if your manic symptoms increase.
- Communicate with loved ones. Let those closest to you know what is going on, and use whatever help they might be able to offer.

CHAPTER 13

Dealing with Depression

I t can be more difficult to spot an oncoming depressive episode than a manic one; the changes can be more subtle. That is why it is important to catalog any signs that seem to signal an oncoming change of mood. As with mania, it is possible to treat a severe depressive episode, but it's easier to treat it before it becomes incapacitating. Time spent learning to recognize and intercept developing mood swings will pay off in terms of fewer disruptions in your life, and fewer hospitalizations. Spend time studying how bipolar disorder affects you in particular to determine if you have a specific pattern of depression warning signs.

Sadness, Mild Depression, and Chronic Depression

Early intervention and medical treatment are the best responses if depression starts to take hold. At the same time, since everyone feels unhappy sometimes, it is important to distinguish between serious chronic depression and mere sadness. Everyone is unhappy sometimes in response to some public or private event or, at times, for no obvious reason. There is, however, an important difference between sadness and depression.

Here is how Emma Parker Bowles, who has bipolar disorder, described her experience with depression in an essay in the *Daily*

Mail: "I can feel when an episode is coming on. And the curse of it is that it is not triggered by anything. I know this is not everyone's experience; for many it is triggered by an event or a devastating loss. For me, I can sense that it is on the horizon, like an animal when an earthquake is about to happen. I try to keep going about my business but everything is overshadowed by feelings of dread and foreboding. I start to feel emptier and emptier, like there is a leaking valve in my soul and it is starting to seep away. Indecision creeps in, concentration creeps away. Everything is bleak and grey."

Sadness

Bowles's experience is clearly different from common sadness, which everyone experiences. Brief periods of sadness are normal and they don't keep people from functioning in other ways. Occasional sadness is part of the balance of a life. When it lasts for many days or weeks, however, it can become pathological.

 Alert

Sadness is not depression. Sadness does not cause you to lose all interest in people and activities, or to withdraw from society. It does not leave you unable to get out of bed, leave your home, or make even the smallest of decisions. It does not wreak havoc on your eating and sleeping habits. Most important of all, sadness does not make you suicidal and obsessed with death.

If you have bipolar disorder and feel sad now and then for a day or so, you may not be showing a symptom of an illness. In fact, it might even signal a healthy mental outlook, since it is normal to feel sad in response to sad events. People with bipolar disorder, however, must be especially careful in distinguishing between feeling a little blue and the beginning of a depressive episode. If you are not sure, check with your doctor or therapist. Keep ahead of your feelings to keep them under control.

Mild and Chronic Depression

Sometimes minor or mild depression can follow specific incidents. Or it can be a lingering condition called dysthymia. Therapy may identify the cause of the depression and antidepressants might be prescribed on a short- or long-term basis, depending on your illness and the practices of your doctor.

Mild depression allows people to function, but half-heartedly. They may seem to be going through the motions, their minds elsewhere. Some studies have raised doubts about the effectiveness of antidepressants prescribed for cases of mild depression but the condition still should be treated if it affects a person's quality of life. Lifestyle changes, therapy, and some medications may be able to relieve symptoms and prevent the condition from getting worse.

Essential

Antidepressant medications may or may not be right for you if you become depressed. Antidepressants by themselves are not an appropriate treatment regimen if you have bipolar disorder. In fact, they can make things much worse by sending you into full-blown mania. Depending on your personal situation and the preference of your doctor, you may be given temporary medications and different long-term medicines to control your moods, including depressive episodes. This is one more reason it is so important to be under a doctor's care for bipolar disorder.

Major, chronic depression goes far beyond sadness. In fact, to sufferers, death might seem the only way to escape from it. You do not have a "good cry" in response to major depression; instead, you might cry uncontrollably, without an obvious cause. Or you might reach a point where you don't bother to cry, as joy, motivation, and a reason for living seems to be sucked out of you.

This is the metaphor Harry Potter author J. K. Rowling, who suffered from depression, used when she created the eerie creatures she called Dementors. These ghostly entities circle, corner, and then paralyze victims as they draw joy from them, leaving despair and depression. They were among the most terrifying threats in a series of books filled with scary magical and mystical creatures.

Major depression is not something you can snap out of by remembering an upbeat saying or forcing yourself to smile. It requires medical intervention.

Preventing Depression

Serious depression can be treated, but it is easier to treat it early. It is important to stay in close contact with your doctor and/or therapist if you are chronically depressed. Still, as with mania, you can try to minimize the likelihood of a depressive episode by taking certain practical measures in your daily life.

Tending Mind and Body

Things will always go less than perfectly and it's normal to gripe a bit when they do, but when negative thoughts become dominant, you are increasing your chances of sliding into depression. It affects your ability to function and can lead to a skewed view of everything in your life. Breaking the cycle of self-defeating thoughts can increase your resilience and your ability to handle setbacks and stress. Cognitive behavioral or other therapy may help you with this.

In addition to doing away with negative thought patterns, there are other things you can do that have been reported to improve mood. Fresh air, exercise, and a balanced diet can help you feel good about yourself. But try to make eating well and exercising fun, not work. Try different exercises and/or find someone to exercise with. Choose activities that interest you. Rather than forcing yourself to go outside, can you find something you enjoy doing indoors, or vice versa? If you truly hate going to a gym, is there some other form of exercise—such as taking long walks—you enjoy more?

You are in charge. Experiment, find what works for you, but get moving before you fall into a slump that gets worse and worse.

Many people benefit from taking up meditation or other relaxation techniques. If you cannot afford classes, use books or tapes from your public library. But take charge and fill your time with healthy habits.

A Well-Paced Life

Remember the advice: Nothing in excess. Try not to do too much or too little. If you are pushing yourself too hard, you might become unhappy, especially if things go wrong after all your effort. You also might wear down your immune system and make yourself vulnerable to physical illness.

By contrast, doing nothing day after day can be depressing for anyone. If you are unable to work outside the home, perhaps there is work you could do at home. Or if unable to work at all, you might be able to take up a craft or hobby that engages your attention. If money is an issue, there is the public library. Become well read or an expert on a given topic. Set a goal such as reading the complete works of a certain author.

 Fact

Even though a solid 80 percent of the people who seek treatment for depression find improvement, the majority of people afflicted by the illness do not seek treatment. Their depression not only keeps them from accomplishing all they could, but negatively affects the people they know and love.

Consider volunteer work. You might meet some good people while doing something that helps others, and remind yourself there can be a deeper purpose for living.

If you work, plan interesting evenings, weekends, and vacations. Open your world to people and things other than yourself.

A Low-Stress Home

Make your home environment—and your work environment, if possible—places that don't promote depression. There are number of simple things you can do.

Keep It Organized and Clean

As previously discussed, a tranquil home can help you feel stable and good about yourself. If possible, have at least one object in each room of your home that makes you happy when you see it.

Some people find that simple touches such as candles, sports memorabilia, photographs, incense, plants, flowers, or a bowl of fresh fruit make a room seem pleasant. Keep reminders of happy times around your home: photos of people and pets you care about, mementos of happy occasions, or other objects that stir pleasant memories and remind you of not being depressed.

⌐. Essential

Sometimes depression develops in the absence of an obvious cause or trigger. In other cases, it may be traced to specific events and factors. Some potential triggers you should know about include alcohol and illegal drugs, stress, major life changes, seasonal changes, and in some cases prescription medications such as corticosteroids.

Clear Away Bad Memories

Don't be reminded of painful memories on a regular basis if you can help it. For example, if you feel unhappy whenever you think of a certain person, do not keep her portrait on display in your home or office, even if you feel you are expected to. If something is broken, either get it fixed or throw it away. If certain music makes you unhappy, do not keep it in your house. The same holds true for books, pictures, or DVDs.

What to Do If You're Depressed

Use all the tools at your disposal to prevent a developing depression from progressing to major depression. Obviously, call your doctor or therapist; her help can ward off an episode.

Some Warning Signs

Losing interest in one activity or event may not mean depression is coming, but when you can't find anything that interests you, take it as an indication that you should start fighting back. Seek out a friend, counselor, or therapist. Get outside, if possible, to exercise. Listen to music. Seek out social activities.

Your depressions might begin with a change in sleep habits, including poor quality or too little or too much sleep. One of your first signs of a problem might be crying for no reason, worrying more than usual, or feeling especially anxious. You might have physical symptoms such as aches, pains, fatigue, or cognitive symptoms such as forgetfulness, distractedness, or slow thinking.

Steps to Fight Oncoming Depression

The NIMH offers some suggestions for dealing with depression before treatment begins to work. They can be just as useful as tactics for resisting a developing depression and getting back to a healthy mood:

- Don't think about taking on large projects; break them down into small steps and pace yourself.
- Don't isolate yourself. Try to be around other people for at least a portion of the day.
- Look at small improvements in your life as big advances. If your sleep or appetite improves but you are still feeling down, recognize it as progress. Your mood will improve with time, effort, and treatment.

- Don't make major, life-changing decisions while you are feeling down. Talk to confidants about your decision to post-pone job changes, marriage, divorce, or other major deci-sions. Hold off until your mood has returned to a more positive state.

Other methods of empowerment that you can employ include:

- List your warning signs. If certain thoughts, moods, sensa-tions, or hunches have signaled the onslaught of depression in the past, write them down and watch for them from now on.
- Know and use what works. If some activities such as talking to certain people, visiting special places, watching certain films, or reading certain books has worked before to improve your mood, use them whenever things start to drag. If they stop working, find replacements for them when you can.
- Find people who cheer you up. If you know people who are good listeners and who have a great deal of empathy, invite them somewhere as your guest or just arrange to talk to them.
- Build a formal support system. Maybe you are part of a local support group or have an online support group. Use these contacts when you feel yourself sliding toward depression. Just make sure you know and trust the people you are depending on for support.

Try to keep up with your daily responsibilities. Feeling con-nected to the outside world will help. Even if you do not work, give yourself errands to run and people to go see before the depression prevents you from doing them.

Avoid negativity whenever possible. Avoid people, places, and things that tend to bring you down. If you are seeing everything in negative terms, talk to your therapist about how you can learn to change your thought patterns with, for example, cognitive behavior therapy.

 Question

Can writing help alleviate feelings of depression?
Yes. Whether it is simply to vent or to create something of interest to other people, try using your unhappy thoughts creatively by writing them down. This can be a journal, a poem, story, play, or novel. The act of writing can distract you somewhat from your depression, and the insights you discover may give you a sense of satisfaction. It doesn't have to be publishable material, although it may be. The first Harry Potter novel was written against a background of the author's depression.

For some people, major depression can hit with the power of an avalanche. You may not be able to "snap out of it" by trying to change your feelings of hopelessness and guilt or overcoming mental sluggishness, but you can still seek help from mental health care professionals and friends. Instead of withdrawing, which is often the first inclination when depression strikes, tell them what you are feeling. They can help you take back control of your thoughts and life.

If Depression Escalates

If, despite your attempts to limit it, your depression worsens, there are other things you can do to protect yourself. Reach out to providers of support, such as the following:

- **Your doctor:** Most psychiatrists have an emergency number or a switchboard that will forward emergency information. While waiting to talk to your doctor, you could also try your psychologist or the facilitator of your weekly support group. If you cannot reach your psychiatrist, you can try your family doctor. Ideally, you will have worked out an arrangement ahead of time with your psychiatrist should he be out of town.

- **Your friends or loved ones:** If you live alone, it might be a good idea to see if you can sleep at a friend's house for the night. The sheer novelty might be refreshing, and maybe your friend can cheer you up. If you are a single parent, perhaps a relative or friend can help temporarily with your children.
- **Suicide hotline and mental health advice:** Find out the Hotline Crisis number for your area by visiting the 24-hour Hotline Numbers State Crisis Lines website at *http://mentalhealth.samhsa.gov/hotlines/state.asp* or *http://suicidehotlines.com/national.html*. Write it down. Program it into your cell phone, keep a copy in your purse or wallet and around your home so it will be easy to find if you need it.
- **911:** You can call 911 and explain that you are feeling dangerously depressed.
- **A hospital:** Another possibility is to check into a hospital. Many medical hospitals have psychiatric wards; those that do not might still be able to send you to one that does.

Major depression is ruthless. It takes away your reason for living. You start to feel hopeless, as if nothing could possibly make a difference. It makes you ask, "Why bother to seek help?" It is crucial that you act as soon as you begin to feel depressed.

Essential

Dial 1-800-273-TALK (8255) or 1-800-SUICIDE (1-800-784-2433) at any hour to get immediate mental health care advice from The National Suicide Prevention Lifeline. You can discuss any mental health concern you have, not just suicidal thoughts. The call is confidential.

Sadly, each year thousands of people reach a point where they do not ask for help, and many of them take their lives. This is especially sad because treatment for major depression is widely recognized as effective. Do not become the next statistic. You are worth saving; you do deserve to find the help you need, and help is available.

It is the job of mental health care professionals to help people who need it. You should never feel guilty about turning to professional services when you need them. Depression can make people want to be isolated, but if you can just hit one button on your phone and speed dial a helpful source, you can get lifesaving help with minimal effort.

Dealing with the Aftermath

In the throes of depression, it can seem as if the weight inside you will never lift. Try focusing on other times in your life when depression—or other problems—seemed insurmountable, but through medication, therapy, and/or your support network it lifted and you survived. That can happen again. Just as in the past, you can get through it and the pain will ease.

 Fact

Depression disables more people across the globe than any other medical condition, according to the World Health Organization. And the incidence of major depressive illness appears to be increasing. In the last twenty years, the incidence of this illness has risen from 3 percent to more than 7 percent.

Once your depression is over, there might be a temptation to belittle yourself. You might feel embarrassed or ashamed. Instead of thinking like this, remember that depression is an illness. Instead of feeling remorse, feel proud of yourself for getting the help you needed—too many people fail to do so. And the people you truly care about are proud of you and happy you are still here, even if they don't tell you in so many words.

If you are a creative person, perhaps through writing, painting, or music you can convey how you feel now that the depression has subsided. Or you can talk about your experiences to those who need to hear them: people with depression, their loved ones, the medical community, and our elected officials who disperse money for research. Your story might give hope to other people and generate public awareness on many levels.

CHAPTER 14

Staying in Control

If you have bipolar disorder or are close to someone who has it, it might feel at times as though your life revolves around this illness. Although a serious mood disorder requires considerable attention, it doesn't have to dominate every thought and action. This chapter offers some suggestions for keeping bipolar disorder from taking over your life.

Learning from Bipolar

If sometimes you are overwhelmed by all the dos and don'ts associated with this condition—the symptoms, medications, and advice about how to live—it can help to remember the far reaching positive effects they have on your life when the condition is under control. Treatment and prevention can have benefits, such as increased self-knowledge and strong incentives to lead a healthier life than most of the population is inclined to lead.

The Positive Aspects of Treatment

If you think of treatment simply as the pills you have to take every day and the follow-up visits to your doctor, try thinking of it in a broader sense. For example, successful treatment of this illness often provides a side benefit of greater self-knowledge. Your experience with the extreme moods of the disorder provides insight into who you are in health compared to who you are in illness. The price of bipolar illness can be extraordinarily high, but if you have managed to get the illness under your control, you have accomplished something on a scale that many people never achieve. Many people never learn much about themselves, and suffer an undefined sense of indecision and dissatisfaction as a result. You have learned the value of health and what can be done with it. Thus, you may be more self-aware than many other people. And if you are in effective therapy, you have opportunities to learn even more about yourself. A close relative of a person with bipolar can also benefit from family or personal therapy.

 Fact

No one who has experienced the pain would choose to have alternating periods of crippling depressions and uncontrolled mania, but pursuing treatment may introduce you to some interesting people. If bipolar disorder had not been a part of your life, you may have missed meeting some people who turn out to be positive influences in your life. Whether they are medical professionals, members of a support group, and/or people who share the illness with you, it is possible that some of your closest friends will emerge from your experience with the disorder.

Effective control of the disorder also provides an incentive to adopt and follow a healthy lifestyle. Eating wisely, practicing relaxation techniques, exercising, developing good sleep habits, staying away from alcohol and illegal drugs . . . all the strategies you have been encouraged to adopt to improve your life by decreasing the occurrence of wild mood swings can make you stronger in ways that go beyond treatment of bipolar disorder. If you take an active part in the effort to master this illness, you can end up knowing quite a lot about nutrition, physical and mental health, the medical profession, and other people. A loved one who is accompanying you on the journey can share similar insights.

Self-discipline can be another benefit. Before treatment, people with this disorder often lead chaotic lives. Successful treatment requires sticking to a regimen. If you combine this with habits that reduce disorganization and clutter in your daily life, you may feel freer. In therapy, you might pick up tips on how to structure your day and plan strategies for accomplishing long- and short-term goals. You may be one of the majority of creative people who is more productive because you have found effective medication for controlling extreme mood fluctuations. Many people—with or without the disorder—struggle to have skills such as these and a sense of order in their lives. These lessons, and even the example you set, can benefit people in your inner circle.

 ## Question

What does your choice in friends say about you?
Some theories of self-identity suggest that how you see yourself is closely related to the type of people you choose to associate with. For example, if you associate mostly with people affected by bipolar disorder, having bipolar is probably the most important part of your identity. If instead you associate mostly with fellow sports fans, your interest in sports is probably a more important element of your identity than bipolar disorder.

Aspects Unaffected by Bipolar

As we have seen, bipolar disorder effectively treated does not have to define you or occupy every second of your life. There are positive or enjoyable things in your life that have nothing to do with the illness. Try making a list of talents, interests, people and things you love that are independent of the disorder. It can include personal tastes: foods, music, hobbies, collectibles, movies, and places you love. Realize that you have a life apart from this condition.

You have interests that are not bestowed on you by a mood disorder. While it is possible that having bipolar disorder can heighten certain creative expressions, you have talents, skills, and abilities that can be developed and flourish if you are inclined to pursue them.

If you are lucky, you also may have people who care about you. If you are alone and you want to reach out, there are health care providers, volunteers, and activists who deeply care. Whether they are family members, friends, or fellow volunteers you have encountered along the way, such relationships can enrich your life and bring meaning to it.

Turn Your Focus to Others

When you are ready, it can help to change your focus from yourself to helping others. Even if you already care for someone with bipolar disorder, there are things you can do for others that might give you a fresh outlook and an even greater sense of accomplishment.

If You Have Bipolar Disorder

Surviving a serious mental disorder provides experience that many people can't understand. For some, it confers a greater ability to empathize with people who are having difficult times. Using this understanding and compassionately sharing it can help you as well as others. If you decide to assist others through a volunteer organization, take on only what you can handle; check with your doctor or therapist to discuss your plans if you are not sure. In just a few hours a week, you might be able to do something that not only helps someone else but helps you forget about your own troubles for a little while. You could become active in a support group or in a network for people with mental disorders and their loved ones.

Of course, the volunteer work you do does not have to be directly related to bipolar disorder. Plenty of people need help in all kinds of areas of their lives. You could read to the blind or deliver food to the elderly. If you don't want to work directly with people, you could volunteer to work behind the scenes in the back office, handling mail, filing, organizing, or helping out as needed for a charity or social or political cause you support.

If you have time and money to spare, you can organize fundraisers for a nonprofit group or simply raise money to make donations yourself.

With or without a job, you might be able to volunteer a little time to give your life more meaning and make yourself feel more productive.

If You Care for Someone with Bipolar Disorder

If you already care for someone who is dealing with bipolar disorder, you might think—understandably—that you already do your share. If anything, you might need to make more time for yourself. As a caretaker, this is a reasonable stance; you must protect yourself from overwork and worry. Burnout is a serious consequence of caring for someone with a serious disease.

You might be one of those, however, who finds that extending your influence makes you feel more satisfied and fulfilled. If you have the time and energy, some form of volunteer work for the disadvantaged, improving your community, or working for a cause you believe in can give you a renewed sense of purpose. If you can make the time and you're inclined to be active, it can help remind you that there is a world beyond your own worries.

You will still need time for yourself, but volunteer work itself may be able to satisfy a bit of your need to get away if it involves working with interesting, equally generous people. This can be a partial solution if you have been spending a lot of time caregiving at the expense of taking care of your own needs.

Learning from Setbacks

In striving to get beyond the challenges presented by bipolar disorder, you may sometimes succeed and at other times fail. You may have relapses despite faithful adherence to your treatment regiment. You may slip while following practices that reduce the risks of episodes. This is a normal part of mastering this disorder. Emphasize resuming your treatment regimen, rather than berating yourself for a temporary setback. Turning negative thinking patterns into positive ones can set a tone in your life that can reduce stress and the chances of having an episode.

Say you haven't worked in a while and you try a new job, which turns out to be too much for you to handle. A short while later, you either quit or are fired. There are many self-defeating things you can think, including:

- It is all my fault.
- It is all their fault.
- I might as well never even try to work again.
- I am an incompetent person.
- Everyone is always out to get me.
- I will never succeed at anything.

Instead of indulging these negative thoughts and conclusions, try instead to determine what you can learn from the experience that will help you in the future. For example: What did you do right at the job and what did you have problems with? Note the things that come easily for you. Maybe there is a job out there that emphasizes those skills or activities.

What can you do to improve your skills to offset the things you had trouble with? Some aspects of the job may have been beyond your level of endurance. Might a little more training or a slightly different outlook allow you to handle similar work in the future? If so, what specific steps can you take to acquire these new skills or attributes? Did you learn anything as a result of your employment that you can use for any reason in the future? There may be larger lessons that you can take away from your experience. Ask yourself:

- **Did you learn more about your strengths and weaknesses?**
  Do you now have a deeper awareness of what sorts of environments you can handle, the kinds of situations you find acceptable, and the types of people you find interesting?
- **Did you learn more about how you relate to other people?**
  Were there people you found easy to talk to? Difficult to talk to? What made the difference? When are you comfortable in social situations, and when are you uncomfortable?
- **Did you learn more about how to present yourself to others?** Do you now know a little more about what is effective and what is not in the job interview process, in talking with the boss, or in dealing with coworkers, clients, or the general public?
- **Did you learn more about how to accept defeat?** No one likes to have something they were looking forward to not work out, but surviving a setback, learning from it, and coming back better prepared is a victory.
- **Did you learn more about how to cheer yourself up?** Since unhappy things happen to everyone, it is a valuable skill to know how to be good to yourself in a healthy way when disappointment strikes.
- **Did you learn more about how to ask others for help?** If you felt embarrassed or ashamed about the job, were you able to get past it and discuss with your support network how you felt? Being able to seek and accept help is another important life skill that can be useful in overcoming bipolar disorder.
- **Did you learn more about how effective your medication is?** If you have wondered sometimes if your medication does or does not have certain effects on your bipolar disorder, did you learn anything more about this from the job?

Losing a job is just one example. The same type of questioning exercises and analysis can apply to other types of situations you are likely to encounter as you go on with life after controlling bipolar disorder.

Accepting Limitations

Some people with bipolar disorder are extremely successful (although many testify to the suffering the illness has caused them and others). They are famous and wealthy. Their treatment appears to be highly effective. Other people are not in the public eye, and therefore not well-known, but just as successful.

Some people with the disorder have more difficulty overcoming it. They might have bipolar I with rapid cycling, for instance, a most serious form of the disorder. Treatment may be partially effective at best. Even if the medication keeps their symptoms under control, its side effects might interfere with other aspects of their lives. In this case, having a realistic sense of your limitations can help you live with bipolar disorder. The same is true for the people who care about you.

Your Own Limitations

It is always possible new, more effective treatments for bipolar disorder will be developed that will help the minority of people who are currently not helped by medications and treatments. In the meantime, you have little choice but to come to terms with what you are able to do and what those around you are able to do.

⌐ Essential

Having multiple roles in life usually means having multiple social networks. While this can make for a busier daily life, it often reduces stress. By having more than one social network to fall back on, people often worry less if there are problems with one of their friends or associates. Thus, there are multiple advantages to having diverse interests.

Keep in mind that nearly everyone has things they wish they were better at, had more time for, remembered to do, etc. If you have had to compromise some or even most of your life goals or daily habits, you are hardly alone. If you did not have bipolar disorder, you would have had to make compromises just the same. Some would undoubtedly have been different, but others would have been the same.

Limitations for Caregivers and Loved Ones

If you are the loved one of a person with bipolar disorder, perhaps you are hard on yourself for not figuring out sooner what the problem was. Or maybe you regret having said or done some things that appear selfish or hurtful in retrospect. You might wish you could do more to help the person—or maybe you worry that you are too protective and do more than you should. When you have to deal with the needs of a person with bipolar disorder and look out for other family members plus your own needs, you might feel as if there is no way for you to do it all.

As a caregiver, you need to remember that you cannot do everything for everyone. Your first priority should be making sure you take care of yourself as best you can through self-help groups, paid assistance if you can afford it, and advice from mental health care professionals. You will not be able to help someone else or yourself if you burn yourself out or suffer a mental or physical health crisis. The situation you find yourself in would be challenging for anyone. Remember that you are not responsible for anyone's mental illness. You cannot heal anyone; you can only help. Whatever you do to help is reason enough for you to feel like you are making a contribution.

Others' Limitations

One of the symptoms of mania is being overly nosy about other people's business. It is best to avoid getting obsessed about what the other people in your life are doing "right" or "wrong." On the other hand, you should speak up if you think someone is, for example, treating you too harshly or treating you like a child. Tell the person directly, and keep the focus on yourself—how you feel, not what the other person should be doing. Inform the person that although you happen to have bipolar disorder, it does not mean that anyone has the right to talk down to you in a demeaning, disrespectful, or insulting manner.

 Fact

> Some counselors advocate the use of "I messages" when dealing with serious issues with a loved one. Rather than saying that "you" did this or that to "me," people are more likely to be receptive when you keep the emphasis upon yourself, rather than assume you know the other person's intentions.

If someone you care about has bipolar disorder, you might wonder at times if the person is copping out—if maybe he could accomplish more or do something differently, but instead is using the disorder as an excuse. If you find yourself feeling this way, get some facts by talking to the person's doctor or therapist. Consult your own advisor, if you have one. Don't let your resentment fester; it will end up hurting both of you.

Setting Goals for the Future

In coming to terms with a challenge such as a major mood disorder, it's useful to forgive past events while learning from them. It's also necessary, if you are going to master this illness, to have realistic goals for the future. Realistic goals can keep you from wasting time obsessing or despairing about things not going as you would like. Realistic goals will also enable you to devote your mental and physical energy to efforts that are more likely to pay off in terms of satisfying accomplishments.

If You Have Bipolar Disorder

With input from your psychiatrist of therapist, think about what you might be able to improve in your life. Start with your outlook and attitude. If there are negative assumptions you make about yourself, others, or certain situations, is it possible to reframe these ideas to make them more productive? Are you seeking out the best therapy you can afford or find?

Alert

The looking glass self is a concept that refers to the ways in which people judge themselves on the basis of how they think others judge them. If you think that other people are impressed by you, you will be impressed by yourself as well. But if you think others are critical of you, there is a tendency for you to be self-critical.

Also consider your job or career. If you do not work, is it possible you could find something to do part time? If you do work, is it something you enjoy, or would you be happier doing something else? If you like what you do, is there a goal you can set for yourself to make your career more engaging?

In terms of your home environment, ask yourself: Do you have a home that makes you feel good when you enter it? What are some realistic, affordable things you can do to make your home nicer?

In terms of diet and exercise: Do you eat balanced meals? Do you get at least some form of regular exercise, even if it is just walking? Would you like to be in better shape, eat better, or stick to a realistic diet? Are your sleep habits likely to reduce stress or do they make you feel tired and irritable?

Your close personal relationships are another very important part of your life. If you do not have a partner and want one, is it a realistic goal to try to find one? If you do have a partner, are there things you can do to improve the relationship? Are there people you would like to get along with better or apologize to? Would you like to change how you deal with certain people?

In terms of personal interests: Do you have an interest or hobby that you enjoy? Is there something you would like to spend time doing that you can afford to do yet you are not doing? Do you ever do volunteer work?

By focusing on a realistic future goal, you do not have to dwell so much on the ways in which bipolar disorder might confine you.

 Fact

> The term "possible selves" refers to how you can mentally imagine yourself taking on different roles from the ones you now have. Often, the new roles you choose are ones that you think will be consistent with the self-image you want to have. Roles that dramatically depart from your current self-image might be chosen as a means to reinvent yourself.

For the Loved One of a Person with the Disorder

If you live with a person with a major mood disorder, you deserve a chance to grow and set personal goals as much as anyone. Depending on the degree of illness of the person you assist, however, you may find this more challenging than others can imagine due to the responsibilities you have as a caregiver.

Your Private Life

Looking after yourself should be high on your priority list. Neglecting your own needs while caring for a loved one is perhaps the most serious potential problem you face. Do most of your thoughts tend to center on the person with bipolar disorder, or can you manage to take some time for your own needs, wants, and relaxation, for your own goals and pursuits? If not, then finding a way to do it can become a goal for you. Pick something small and specific to start, even if it is just a few minutes set aside for you each day.

Your goal might be to ensure that you eventually achieve a rewarding private life. Try to keep a list of tasks and activities that are just for you. It will remind you that you have a responsibility to yourself. However, slowly and despite starts and stops, try to build on the things you include on your personal to-do list. Accept setbacks as part of the process; during one week you may not make significant progress in your efforts to make time for yourself. The next week may offer more opportunities if you persist. Don't give up. Keep what works and change what doesn't.

Essential

Family or psychoeducation programs help people who care for and/ or live with someone with a mental disorder as well as the patient. The insights and understanding provided by this kind of therapy have been shown to improve the mental health of both parties.

Building a social support network is another way to lower the risk of caregiver burnout. You might include fellow members of a support group, friends, and people who share a common interest aside from mental illness.

Your Health

Whatever time you can devote to your health, as well as to your private life, will help you handle stress better and decrease the chances you will face demoralizing medical problems. The time and effort it takes to schedule a yearly physical exam, eat nutritious foods, limit junk food, exercise regularly, and get enough rest will pay for itself if it makes you better able to handle stress. Counseling or therapy just for you is also worth considering. A competent therapist can help you figure out ways to handle the challenges you face.

Finally, include relaxation on your list of goals; you cannot be stressed and relaxed at the same time. Any healthy form of relaxation will temporarily reduce your stress and provide a mini break or mini vacation. If you can eventually manage to introduce regular stress-reducing periods into your life, it is possible to carry the relaxation over into other, more stressful, times of the day.

CHAPTER 15

If You Know Someone Who You Think Is Bipolar

A person with bipolar disorder who has not been diagnosed or who is untreated poses a serious problem, as she has the potential to destroy her life, disrupt the lives of those around her, and harm herself or others. It's important to take responsible action if you believe that someone you know has untreated bipolar disorder. Getting that help may not be easy, but if you care about the person, you will probably try. You may succeed, but you shouldn't blame yourself if you don't.

Look at Yourself First

Before taking action, it is useful to look closely at your motivation: Why do you think this person has bipolar disorder, and are you prepared to deal with it?

Explore Your Motives

You many know someone who has widely, unpredictably fluctuating moods. Sometimes he can be likeable, but other times he gets angry, arrogant, or withdrawn without warning or explanation. You get angry and frustrated because the mood shifts seem so unjustified. Their unpredictability puts you on edge. You find yourself wanting to avoid this person—although, depending on your relationship, this feeling might make you feel guilty. And even as you are angry with him, you feel sorry for him. If you ever tried to aggressively confront the person when he seemed unreasonable, you probably regretted it. Nothing seems to help.

Whatever the cause of this person's problem—physical, mental, or emotional—it is important to approach the situation with compassion.

Fact

In helping others, people often employ the minimax strategy. This means that people try to determine how they can help the most by exerting the least amount of effort. For example, calling 911 when someone is having a psychotic break or other serious episode takes just a moment, and will probably be more useful than trying to alter the behavior without knowing what you are doing.

It is normal to have mixed feelings about a person with extreme mood fluctuations that are often directed at you. You might even feel as though you hate the person at times. Try to remember that the person's problem could be beyond her control, and in the case of a mental disorder like bipolar disorder, it unquestionably is.

It won't help anyone if you try to settle any scores or approach the matter with the intention of punishing the person for all the unhappiness her behavior has caused. It won't help her if you try to prove that you were right all along. You will be much more successful in helping this person, and ultimately yourself, if your motive is to lead her to treatment, rather than to prove a point.

Prepare for a Struggle

Be ready for challenges if you decide to get involved. First, you may have to do it alone. You may be the only person who recognizes or admits that the troubled individual needs to see a doctor. If this is the case, you will have to try hard to stand by your convictions if you want to succeed. It is also possible that others agree the person needs help, but you are the only one who is willing to get involved. In this case, you might feel resentment toward the people who could be helping but aren't. Doing it by yourself means you will be dealing with the added difficulty of lacking practical or emotional support.

On the other hand, you might receive unwanted help. Just as frustrating as having to do it alone is getting help from someone who is not good at it. For example, maybe your helper has very poor communication skills and neither listens well nor speaks well. In this case, you might be better off trying to do the job by yourself.

Be ready if the person you are trying to help misinterprets or resists your efforts. If someone has never seen a psychiatrist or is highly defensive, she may resent your interference and insist that nothing is wrong, that it is none of your business or that you are the one with a problem. You may have to back off if you face a bullying or threatening response.

Essential

Mania sometimes appears in patients with brain tumors, Huntington's disease, multiple sclerosis, and epilepsy. Patients with strokes or serious head injuries might also undergo manic episodes. A thorough physical exam should be included in any initial psychiatric examination.

Keep in mind the possibility that you might be wrong. Since you are not a psychiatrist conducting a formal evaluation, you should be prepared for the possibility that this person will not be diagnosed with a mental disorder. Because you might be misreading the situation, it is important that you express your concern in an unemotional, sensitive manner. It isn't wrong to express concern even if you are wrong. At least you cared enough to show her you wanted to help her when she was distressed.

When to Intervene

Many people say they come from a dysfunctional family. The claim is so common it seems to be in danger of losing its significance. Remember, however, if you think someone has bipolar disorder, it is not a pop psychology game; it is an extremely serious matter. Even though you are not a psychiatrist, you can still look for signs that indicate someone could benefit from a consultation with a professional health care provider.

Is the Person Having an Episode?

If someone you know has full-blown manic-depressive episodes, try to get help for him now. Even if he is not having an episode at the moment and seems fine, this period of normalcy will not last if the problem is bipolar disorder. If he seems to have more minor episodes of mania or depression, remember that if left untreated these symptoms can develop into more serious forms of bipolar disorder; bipolar II can progress to bipolar I, the more serious and most difficult to treat form of bipolar disorder.

Many people believe that a person with a substance abuse problem must "hit bottom" before she is ready for help. This does not apply to people with mood disorders. Someone in the midst of mania or depression may not understand what is happening to him. He has no power to turn off the episode and avoid its effects.

Even people who have been diagnosed and treated sometimes decide in the moment that nothing is wrong during mania or that nothing can be fixed during depression. Of course, plenty of people with undiagnosed bipolar disorder seek treatment on their own, but many do not. This is one time when it is appropriate to mind someone else's business, and try to get him evaluated.

If the person lives with a spouse or relative, involve her, but if he lives alone, someone should intervene before something tragic happens. It could be that the only person is you.

Is the Person Breaking the Law?

Attempting suicide, assaulting another person, stealing, speeding, creating a public disturbance, and lewd conduct are among the more common ways that someone might break the law during a bipolar episode. (Although some people do not know it, it is illegal to attempt or commit suicide.) The police should be called when any of these crimes are committed. Ideally, this will lead to the person getting treatment.

 Alert

The often high rate of risky sexual activity among people with bipolar disorder makes them more likely to acquire sexually transmitted diseases or experience unwanted pregnancy than the general population. Other symptoms associated with bipolar disorder can lead to a distorted belief or indifference about safe sexual practices.

If you report to the police someone you think has bipolar disorder, or if you know she has been arrested—you should not assume the police will make sure she is seen by a psychiatrist. Instead, inform the police that she has a history of highly erratic behavior and should be seen by a psychiatrist. Then follow up and see if this has happened. It is also a good idea to report what you know to her attorney—if she has one—or to help her obtain the services of an attorney if she needs them.

Expressing Your Concerns

If someone you think is ill has come to the attention of the police but has not broken the law, the police may or may not assist in getting an involuntary psychiatric assessment. If they don't, you can still try to arrange help. One of the first things you can do in your quest to have a loved one evaluated by a professional is to express your concerns, starting with other people who care about this person.

Talk to the Family

If the person has family or loved ones, find out if any of them agree with you. Perhaps you can form an alliance to help each other and the person in need. See if together you can form a plan to help him.

Convincing other people, of course, is not always easy. For one thing, you could be wrong. But assuming that you have good reason to think someone has bipolar disorder, it will help your case if you do the following:

- Make it clear that you are not judging nor blaming. Explain you are someone who cares and who is making the observation that someone needs help.
- Refer to traits or symptoms of bipolar disorder. Supply examples. Clearly restate the features of mania and depression and, in a nonaccusatory manner, cite instances when he showed clear signs of mood disorder.
- Avoid diagnosing bipolar disorder or other mental illness. Stick to the symptoms and say it is possible to get help and control the troubling behaviors he is showing.
- Pre-empt expected doubts. For instance, you might say in advance, "It isn't that he has been working too hard or feeling happy about being divorced. This is way beyond that, and it's been going on for a long time."
- Give the other people a chance to respond. Don't dominate the conversation. Seek out the observations and feelings of the people you are trying to recruit. Let them think about what you have said. You may be telling them more than they can immediately handle.
- Have a plan. If the other people agree that the person in question might benefit from seeing a psychiatrist, they might think there is nothing they can do about it. It can be helpful if you can say you talked to a doctor or clinic. Then summarize what you learned after speaking with a professional.

Talk to the Person Directly

You might decide it could help to talk to him directly about the symptoms of mood disorders and why you think he should see a doctor. By now, you know he may respond by feeling insulted, embarrassed, angry, or violated, no matter how carefully you phrase your concerns. If you are willing to risk this for the sake of your friend or loved one, there are several issues to consider.

One is whether you should approach him alone or with others. If he is a spouse or best friend with whom you are especially close, it might work if you talked one on one. In other cases, it might be helpful to talk to him in the presence of one or more of his close friends or relatives, but try to avoid the appearance of ganging up on him. Concentrate to expressing concern.

If it very important that you know your facts. Have a list of symptoms handy to help convince him that treatment might be a good idea.

 Fact

The boomerang effect refers to what happens when the listener ends up thinking or doing the opposite of what the speaker intended. One of the main causes of the boomerang effect in human interactions is mistrust of the speaker. Make sure the person you are trying to convince trusts you before you sit down with him.

Consider her state of mind before you begin your discussion. Reasoning with a person in the middle of a severe manic or depressive episode is unlikely to work. When he seems capable of listening to you, be sure you have a concrete and practical plan. If he agrees to get help, conclude by saying, "I'm so glad. Here is the phone number of a good doctor. Let's call him right now." You also could offer to give him a ride to the doctor.

Formal Interventions

If you are convinced that talking to someone directly or to her friends or relatives is not the best plan, you might need to take more formal steps. These can include a group intervention or legal steps to have a person ordered into treatment by the court.

Group Intervention

A group intervention involves a group of concerned individuals sitting down with a person and explaining why they feel she desperately needs help. Often, this is done when addiction or other kinds of compulsive behavior is the problem. It can also be done when mood disorders are suspected. The goal of an intervention is for it to end with the person leaving immediately for treatment. In the case of bipolar disorder, this means she sees a doctor that same day, whether in a hospital or in private practice. Obviously, this requires advanced planning. If the result of the intervention is a promise to make an appointment to see a psychiatrist, it hasn't succeeded, since so much could happen before the appointment is kept, if it ever is.

The intervention should be run by a professional facilitator with experience in handling bipolar disorder—not just milder conditions—and who knows where the person might go for immediate evaluation.

Legal Intervention

If it is obvious that someone needs immediate treatment to protect themselves or others, you might need to take the matter to court. This is a last-resort option that may evoke volatile emotions. The ill person might, for example, scream in your face that she hates you and will never forgive you. This could be highly stressful for you and you might benefit from therapy or counseling after such an experience. But in the final analysis, it is a preferable option to standing by and allowing someone who clearly needs help to harm herself or others.

The laws and procedures for forcing someone to undergo psychiatric evaluation and care vary across states. You can contact your local psychiatric crisis center or speak to an attorney to find the best way to proceed.

Essential

In some states, it is possible to assign someone's disability payments to a relative or health care professional to ensure that the person receives treatment for a mental disorder. The person given responsibility for finances is obligated to give it to the patient only upon proof that she is receiving treatment.

At least one medical doctor must agree that someone has a diagnosable illness that requires immediate treatment. If the court agrees with this assessment, there are numerous possible outcomes, including:

- **Legal guardianship:** You or someone else might be appointed legal guardian. This means that he is deemed incompetent to make his own decisions. In this way, the guardian can order him to receive treatment. Should he refuse treatment, he can be hospitalized at the guardian's request.
- **Outpatient commitment:** The patient agrees to a treatment plan, and can live at home as long as she abides by it. Failure to do so results in hospitalization.
- **Benevolent coercion:** The patient is given a choice between being hospitalized and agreeing to treatment on an outpatient basis. It is similar to outpatient commitment, but it is presented as a matter of choice.
- **Inpatient commitment:** He is committed to a hospital for treatment. This often transpires when other options have failed.

Dealing with the Aftermath

Whatever the outcome of your attempt to help the patient by getting him diagnosed and treated, your work probably has not ended. The personal dynamic between you and the person who needs help has changed. Your relationships with his relatives and friends also may have changed.

Changed Relationship(s)

As a result of your efforts, the person you tried to help may have been diagnosed with a mental disorder, or he may still be undergoing evaluation. It is also possible that a doctor found no evidence of illness.

Some people may be grateful for your efforts to help. Others may be unhappy with you no matter what the outcome is. If close friends or relatives are upset with you, try letting emotions cool. Perhaps their feelings will change over time, and you will able to re-establish close ties with them. If these people were casual acquaintances, you might find it easier to simply move forward without them.

You may receive initial resentment or worse from the person you tried to help. If he eventually is successfully treated, the resentment may (but not necessarily will) change to gratitude. Give it a lot of time.

If the person was not diagnosed with an illness that requires treatment, it is less likely that time will repair your relationship. You will have to remind yourself that the behavior and suffering you saw inspired you to try to help, even if the effort is never appreciated.

How You See Yourself

You may not be quite the same person you were before you became involved. It might be useful to join a support group or see a therapist to help you adjust to these changes if they bother you. Whether you have become everyone's hero or everyone's villain, it is important to keep what other people think of you in perspective.

Protect Yourself

Being in the company of someone you think has a serious mental condition that is not being treated is highly stressful. Efforts—successful or otherwise—to get the person diagnosed are unlikely to go as smoothly as you had hoped. Tension may be further heightened by the realization that it may not be safe for you to be around this person.

Give Yourself Space

The first priority of a rescuer is to protect the rescuer. You will never be able to help anyone if you are physically or emotionally incapacitated. Do not sacrifice your own life or goals for someone else if you want to help her. That is not the same as deciding consciously to change you life or goals to stay and help someone, but make sure it is your choice. Otherwise, you are likely to become bitter and disappointed. The stress you can experience as a caregiver can seriously affect your health particulary if you feel trapped.

If you have relatively few connections to a person with bipolar disorder, yet the situation is so stressful that it is causing you to neglect other important areas of your life, you might decide to sever your ties, at least for the time being. You need to make sure you are eating, sleeping, tending to your loved ones, and doing your job. It is pointless for your life to be as severely compromised as the person who needs help.

Value Your Safety

On occasion, mania can result in acts of vandalism and even violence toward other people. If your gut feeling convinces you that someone close to you has untreated bipolar disorder, ask yourself why you persist in living under the stress. Always remember that you are doing nothing wrong when you protect yourself from a situation that can result in harm to you.

It is always a good idea to have a well-charged cell phone on your person. It can be used to call for help whenever you are threatened in any situation in or out of your home. If you spend a good deal of time with someone who has untreated bipolar disorder, it will be available to summon help for her as well as for you if the need arises. If the person has a psychiatrist, speed dial his number into your phone.

 Fact

> More than half of the people imprisoned in the U.S. have some kind of mental illness, according to the U.S. Department of Justice. Of the estimated 63,000 ill people, more than 32,000 did not receive health treatment before being arrested. Only around one in three state prisoners and one in four federal prisoners who suffer from mental illness receive treatment while behind bars.

If the person seems to be having a manic episode in your presence, remove yourself from the situation if you feel threatened. If you sense that you, the patient, or a third party is in any danger at all, remove yourself and the third party from the patient. Call 911 immediately, then call the patient's doctor if she has one.

CHAPTER 16

If You Know Someone Who Has Bipolar Disorder

If someone in your life has been diagnosed with bipolar disorder, his ability to stick with treatment—and the success of the treatment—will be crucial factors in your relationship. There are other factors you can influence that will enable you to take the best possible care of yourself.

Life with a Spouse with Bipolar Disorder

Living with a person with bipolar disorder can be rewarding if treatment is successful, as it is in the overwhelming majority of cases. Until or unless treatment is effective, however, the experience can drive you to a point where you feel you cannot cope.

Treatment Is Working

If your partner responds well to treatment and does not rebel against staying on medication, then bipolar disorder might seem no different from other treatable medical conditions. In this best-of-all-possible scenarios (short of a cure), bipolar disorder does not ruin your life or your partner's life. You will not be free of problems, of course, since all relationships have problems at times. If treatment works, your problems will not revolve around bipolar disorder nearly exclusively as they most certainly would otherwise.

When Treatment Is Partially Effective

Life will be more complex if your partner's medication is only partially effective. In addition to less than complete control of mood fluctuations, you might have to deal with some complications that can be traced to the partially effective medications. The possibility of a full-scale episode is much more of a reality. You can reasonably expect the subject of bipolar disorder to be a topic of frequent conversations. Issues such as symptoms, medications, side effects, and doctor visits will take up your time.

Most people find they can be annoyed by the idiosyncrasies of other people sometimes. But in this situation, it might be difficult to know when the source of a problem is bipolar disorder and when it is a personality quirk. If, for example, your partner talks too much and interrupts others when they try to interject, is it hypomania (which might not be controllable) or is it simple rudeness (which is controllable)? A therapist's or doctor's opinion might help you answer questions like this.

Essential

See if a doctor or other mental health professional will help you develop an advance directive/relapse prevention plan or an emergency contingency plan in the event a mood gets out of control. Such written guidelines will provide clear steps to take in the event of an emergency, including who and how to contact for help.

Work might also be an issue. Your partner may not be able to work much or at all, and this may put a burden on you. Or maybe your partner tries to work, but can't keep a job. Disagreements about money are a common source of conflict among many couples, but in your situation, the problem may be complicated by the lingering effects of a serious mood disorder.

If you have children, you will need to balance their needs with your partner's needs. As your children get older, they may start helping you with your spouse, which at times you will appreciate. At other times, however, you may feel remorse that they have to deal with a parent with special needs.

No one can decide for you if the relationship is worth maintaining. As with any other marriage or domestic arrangement, you need to weigh the plusses and minuses along with the responsibilities involved. In fairness to your partner, it is not her fault that she and her doctor haven't found the right combination of medications yet. However, if you fear for your safety because of your partner's mood swings, leaving the relationship should not make you feel guilty. If treatment remains only partially effective, there is no guarantee that you will not feel threatened again.

Alert

Various side effects to medication or the possibility of an episode might place limits on your activities as a couple. You may need to avoid some pastimes that you enjoy. There might be times you end up not doing something you had looked forward to because of your partner's unexpected manic or depressive episode. You might often feel the need to acquiesce to your spouse in hopes of avoiding a dramatic mood swing. Support groups and therapists may help you develop strategies for coping with situations like this.

Living Without Treatment

If your partner does not respond to medication, cannot tolerate the side effects, or refuses to take it, you are faced with a very serious situation. If your partner tried medication but it did not work, it might seem sad or unfair to part ways. Unfortunately, it might be the only option to ensure your physical safety as well as your own mental well-being. If there are children involved, their emotional and physical safety must also be taken into consideration.

Some people naively believe that with enough love, symptoms of mental disorders can be modulated or controlled. While you might have a positive influence, in the final analysis, you cannot keep the symptoms of a condition like bipolar disorder from afflicting your partner.

When mania strikes, your savings might vanish if you do not take steps to protect them. Rampant sexual activity with strangers might occur. Thus, some of the most volatile issues couples face under normal conditions—money and sex—are likely to become issues while dealing with untreated bipolar disorder. If your partner falls into heavy depression, you might be so fearful of what she might do that you may not be able to do or think about much else.

Essential

Men whose wives have bipolar disorder might need to make more of an effort to develop a support system. In general, women are more likely than men to have a support system outside of the nuclear family unit. Thus, a woman whose husband has bipolar disorder is more likely to have people she can readily turn to for advice, conversation, and comfort.

Whatever happens in your relationship, consider attending some support groups and counseling sessions for yourself. You want to avoid becoming either an overly controlling or ineffectual partner to your struggling spouse. Your children also may benefit from talking to a professional. The more you learn about the disorder, the better prepared you will be to make decisions regarding you spouse, your family, and yourself.

Life with a Parent with Bipolar Disorder

As a child of someone with bipolar disorder, you might experience a role reversal that leaves you feeling more like the parent than the child. Success or failure with treatment can have a huge impact on how this relationship evolves.

When Treatment Works

A parent responding successfully to medication can be as good a parent as any other. If he is a flawed parent, there is a good chance the reasons are unrelated to bipolar disorder. Some people who have struggled and gained control over physical and mental challenges develop greater insight, sensitivity, understanding, and empathy. When these often rare positive qualities are applied to parenting, children benefit. Furthermore, if the parent who has controlled his bipolar disorder has a special talent or skill, he can be a creative mentor for the child.

Even in this best-case scenario, children should know what bipolar disorder is when they are old enough to understand. They should be aware of the importance of treatment, and also be taught how to handle certain kinds of emergencies should they ever occur.

When Treatment Is Partially Effective

When treatment fails to completely control mood swings, children will need to be reminded often that the episodes they witness are not their fault. Children may feel responsible for events involving family life such as marital strife, divorce, illness, and tragedy that are, in fact, outside their control. They sometimes feel if only they did not make their parent angry or if they were better children, none of the frightening or confusing behavior would happen. Younger children might not understand there is nothing they can say that will make their parent snap out of mania or depression. Counseling and support groups can be especially important for children exposed to this type of anxiety.

Children may share some good times with a parent between episodes, but these good times can be tainted if the parent, for example, later belittles the child in an episode of mania or hypomania or frightens the child by displaying suicidal despair. When mature enough, a child will need to learn the difference between the symptoms of bipolar disorder and the parent's otherwise normal range of behavior.

At the same time, it is best not to overburden the child or expect too much from her. It is hard enough for adults to fully understand a loved one's symptoms. Adults sometimes express frustration, hurt, or anger when dealing with someone's bipolar disorder. Children should have the same latitude to express their feelings. Family therapy has been shown to be very helpful in such situations. It increases understanding and provides hints for coping with difficult situations.

 Fact

An estimated 25 percent of child abuse and neglect in the United States involves mental illness of a parent or primary caregiver. Abusive behavior includes physical, sexual, or emotional abuse. Neglect refers to a failure to meet the basic needs of the child in regard to food, shelter, safety, and education.

Not Receiving Treatment

Parents who do not know they have bipolar disorder might feel guilty about what they put their children through as they struggle with their illness. The same may be true if a parent knows he has bipolar disorder but his medication does not work or its side effects prevent him from taking it.

If a parent could benefit from medication and chooses not to take it, his competency to parent is questionable. The courts might need to intervene, to either force the parent to accept treatment or find a more appropriate home for the children. If you are aware of a child in such an environment, it is your duty to report the situation to social services or others in a position to protect the child exposed to a parent with untreated bipolar disorder.

The presence of a second parent could potentially provide a buffer between the children and the possibly traumatic effect of seeing untreated bipolar disorder, but it doesn't guarantee the physical and emotional health of the children.

Children may understand intellectually that the extreme mood swings they see are the result of illness, but they will still be troubled by them. Communication among family members is crucial. It is a mistake to assume a child feels a certain way without listening to the child. The family should communicate informally and also explore the benefits of doing so in a professional setting.

Life with a Sibling with Bipolar Disorder

Having a brother or sister with bipolar disorder can be a source of minor or major tension, depending on relationships in the nuclear family. How close are you to this sibling? Did she have the disorder when you were growing up? Was it diagnosed and treated? If the bipolar symptoms manifested instead in young adulthood, how much did this impact your own life? Did you live under the same roof at this time?

Treatment Is Working

If your sibling was treated successfully for bipolar disorder as a child, you may have been spared serious difficulty. There might have been instances before diagnosis that were extremely upsetting for you. You may have felt ignored as your sister received attention for acting out such dramatic mood swings and inappropriate behavior. You may have felt guilt for being angry at your sibling, for being ashamed around your friends, or for having been spared from having the same problem. Perhaps other family members continue to give your sibling much more attention than you receive, or you might have resented the help you were expected to provide to your sister.

Children can assume unjustified guilt in other ways. For example, you might feel guilty for not recognizing your sibling had a mental disorder if it wasn't diagnosed. Additionally, if your sibling was punished too severely for behavior beyond her control, you might feel extremely sad for her.

In cases where the bipolar symptoms did not emerge until young adulthood, you might have been unprepared to deal with it all. And even though you are older, you still might resent the attention your sibling gets.

 Alert

> The causes of sibling abuse in families can include lack of parental supervision or ignorance of children's activities, giving older children inappropriate adult responsibilities, favoring one child over another, not stopping violent behavior, and assuming that the behavior is an acceptable manifestation of sibling rivalry.

If your sister is responding well to treatment, and you feel comfortable doing it, try discussing with your family the experience and the effects it had on you. Both informally and in therapy settings, you can work to gain a better understanding of what each of you has been through.

Treatment Is Partially Effective

If you are close to your family, you might find yourself having to help provide care if a sibling is able to control some but not all symptoms of bipolar disorder. This could range from checking on her now and then to being a daily source of support. Some people may not mind doing this, while others might resent it.

At times, you might tire of providing this support. You might feel as though you are sacrificing too much of your life because you never know when you might get a call that your sister is hypomanic or dangerously depressed again. Your resentment may be greater if you feel you are doing more than other close relatives.

Even if you are not very involved in the sibling's everyday life, you might resent the attention she gets or despair over the way others treat her.

Of course, you are not responsible for the mental illness or the fact the medication cannot control it. You can, however, try to help when you can without overstressing yourself. It is natural to feel conflicted in such a situation. The stronger you make yourself by understanding your reaction to your sibling's illness, your feelings for your sibling, and the limits you are willing to go to help will give you a greater sense of control over your own life.

Not Receiving Treatment

If your sibling does not receive treatment, there is a good chance she will be hospitalized multiple times. The best scenario in this case is that she has some means of maintaining a source of food and shelter, whether it is provided by family, public assistance, or her own resources (if she is one of those who built a successful career before the episodes became extreme). The worst scenario would be homelessness, a fate that befalls many people with untreated mental disorders.

Essential

A person is not the disease they have been diagnosed with. A patient with cancer is not a cancer person; he is a person who has cancer. She should not be defined by an illness, no matter how dominating or devastating it is. It might seem to be a pedantic or trivial point, but such labels can have a significant effect on how we regard others and how they regard themselves. A person with bipolar disorder is a complex human being with many other aspects to their character than the phrase "bipolar person" implies.

If you're in the position of caring for your sibling with bipolar disorder as a parent would, then effectively you are no longer siblings, but parent and child. You should seriously consider alternate strategies for the care of your sibling if you are uncomfortable taking on the role of parent.

Life with Relatives
Who Have Bipolar Disorder

You might interact with extended relatives such as grandparents, aunts, uncles, and cousins frequently or rarely, depending on the nature of your family relationships, geography, and opportunity. If any of them has bipolar disorder, the degree to which they impact your daily life may depend entirely on these factors.

Treatment Is Working

If a relative you rarely see is being successfully treated for bipolar disorder, you probably seldom think about it. It is possible that you have a distant relative, a cousin for example, who is in this category. But in some families, extended relatives are closer than in other families. Aunts, uncles, cousins, and grandparents may be seen at least once a week, perhaps even once a day. There might be little difference between cousins and siblings in such families.

In this case, a relative's well-being is more likely to be important to you personally, but as long as the person is responding well to treatment, your burden is probably a light one.

 Fact

Family therapy is often recommended for the treatment of bipolar disorder. Young or old, family members meet with a professional therapist to learn about bipolar disorder, its effects on people, and ways to improve problem-solving skills and communication within the family.

Treatment Is Partially Effective

If an extended relative has bipolar disorder, is only partially helped by treatment, and is someone you are close to, you may have to sort through many of the same issues as you would if he were your sibling or parent. If, on the other hand, the relative is someone whom you seldom have to see, you are probably not affected much by his illness.

Not Receiving Treatment

If you are especially close to a relative who is not receiving treatment, you will be as emotionally invested in his situation as you would be if a member of your immediate family was affected, assuming you are close to your immediate family. The same issues and concerns surrounding his care or commitment may end up involving you. If you assume the responsibility and burden of care, you are just as entitled to therapy and group support as anyone in a similar situation.

Life with a Friend with Bipolar Disorder

Friends are people we choose to know. For some people, friends become their real family—they become closer to these nonrelatives than to their blood kin. Such a friend with bipolar disorder can play just as important a role in your life as a relative who has the disorder.

Treatment Is Working

Since bipolar disorder is often diagnosed in young adults, there is a chance your friend was diagnosed and receiving successful treatment by the time you met her. You might know about the need for checkups and medication, and you may have heard about some of the misadventures experienced before diagnosis. The net effect on your relationship with your friend is minimized by the successful treatment.

If you have known your friend since childhood, you were probably concerned by some of the behavior you witnessed before she was diagnosed. If you had a healthy relationship, it would have come as a relief to learn that the behavior had a name and could be treated.

If, however, you were attracted to your friend while she was experiencing manic episodes and you found it "different" or "exciting," you might have become less interested once treatment began. If that is the case, you may want to look at how and why you go about choosing your friends.

Treatment Is Partially Effective

If your friend's treatment works for some symptoms but not others, you will need to decide how much you want to be involved with her. If you genuinely care about the person—if she is like family—and the lingering symptoms do not cause you to compromise your own life, you might be able to help and provide support. By all means, take advantage of support groups or therapy sessions, especially if the friend is someone you see frequently.

Essential

Having friends may contribute to longevity. Studies show that people who are socially isolated are 25 to 35 percent more likely to die sooner than people with strong support networks. Since today more than twice as many people are living alone than fifty years ago, friends are an especially valuable resource.

If your friendship is strained, however, and you are troubled by your friend's behavior, you might consider distancing yourself, particularly if it threatens your security in any way. Your friend will not be able to simply stop these behaviors, and if you are not willing to accept the inevitable occurrence from time to time, you will have to move on. If this person depends on you but you cannot handle it anymore, you might feel better if you try to find her some other support. You might contact a relative or refer the matter to social services.

Not Receiving Treatment

If you have a friend who has bipolar disorder but is not receiving treatment, make certain that you do not get involved in any manic-inspired activities that threaten your well-being. If your friend feels insulted or betrayed because you do not want to waste your money, have high-risk sex, go without eating or sleeping, or if he does not permit you to disagree with him, blame the illness and go your own way.

If your friend is deeply depressed, he might avoid you and everyone else. You might want to make sure he is safe if you have not heard from him for a while, but you also need to remember that you cannot cure him or make his depression vanish. It is enough that you try to get help for him.

In the absence of a family member or professional, you might need to take it upon yourself to make sure your friend is hospital-ized, if and when it becomes necessary for his own safety. He will need professional care; you need to be prepared for some difficult times if you become part of his inner circle.

Life with a Boss or Coworker with Bipolar Disorder

If you work side by side with someone who has or appears to have bipolar disorder, the characteristic emotional highs and lows will have a special meaning for you. At some point, you may have to deal with a difficult situation that could affect your job or career.

Bipolar disorder does not affect everyone's ability to work in the same way. Some people will have more problems with some tasks than others. Some people may need accommodations at work and others won't. It depends on the type of bipolar disorder, the efficacy of their medication, and the nature of the job.

Treatment Is Working

If someone you work with or for is receiving successful treat-ment for bipolar disorder, you may never know it. Indeed, there is no reason for you to know. Having gotten control of her mood swings, she may be a better boss or coworker because of her strug-gle with the disorder. Ideally, if she has an energetic personality, she has a job that is high on creativity and variety and low on repetition.

There may be some tasks she has trouble completing, but in any work situation there are people who do certain things better than others. And of course, she occasionally might need a long lunch hour for a doctor's appointment. Like many people in a work setting, someone with bipolar disorder might need time off to see to personal business or concerns surrounding her health.

If the illness is under control, issues you might have with this boss or coworker are likely to be unrelated to bipolar disorder.

Treatment Is Partially Effective

A good work environment is tolerant of an employee's disability, including bipolar disorder. But as anyone who has ever held a variety of jobs knows, not all work environments are good.

Lack of sympathy for someone affected by bipolar disorder symptoms in the workplace would not be unusual. If some people think a coworker is not doing her job and making their job harder, they will resent the perceived burden and eventually complain. The boss may be even less sympathetic to a worker whose manic episodes make her inefficient and difficult to work with and whose depressive episodes cause her to miss work entirely.

 Fact

Employers are not allowed to ask job candidates if they have disabilities. If an employer requires a medical examination, it must be given to all applicants. Should a potential employee be shown to have a disability, it must be demonstrated how the disability will prevent him or her from performing the job in order to disqualify the candidate.

Even if glimpses of bipolar disorder do not cause a person to be fired, she might quit in a moment of manic arrogance or impatience. Similarly, depression can make someone abruptly quit or just not show up for work, in an attempt to escape from everyone and everything. A boss with bipolar disorder whose treatment is only partially effective might at times want to work everyone way beyond normal limits. He might set unrealistic goals. Or if medication can't control his depression, the boss might be unavailable when his workers need him.

Not Receiving Treatment

Even if she owns the business enterprise, a boss with untreated bipolar disorder is likely to be out of a job before long. Depression can make the person dangerously unavailable and ineffective, and mania can cause her to make misguided or inappropriate business decisions if she cannot concentrate on the job.

If the boss owns the company or is related to the owner, the firm may suffer a high turnover in staff. Many people will find it difficult to work for this person for long. While any business is vulnerable to failure, there is an especially good chance a business owner with untreated bipolar disorder will go out of business.

Accommodating a Worker with Bipolar Disorder

Whether you supervise or work beside someone with bipolar disorder, there are some things you can do to help them and, perhaps, yourself. The Job Accommodation Network (*www.jan.wvu.edu/media/Bipolar.html*) provides some guidelines for accommodating workers with mental disabilities.

If you have the authority, you can provide ways to help someone keep going throughout the work day by offering work breaks when needed, flexible scheduling, self-pacing, work-from-home options, extra time to master new skills, and time off for doctors' or therapist visits.

It may help some people to decrease unnecessary distractions and work in an out-of-the-way place where they can do their job with few disturbances. Assignments may become less stressful when broken down into smaller tasks with multiple, defined goals.

Providing positive feedback helps all workers, not just those with disabilities. The same is true for providing clear, written instructions regarding goals and, if necessary, suggestions for completing them. Making sure your expectations are clearly stated and understood can help decrease stress in employees who are particularly sensitive to it.

Encouraging frank, open communication can also head off work-related crises before they occur.

As a coworker, you can help by sharing hints for completing tasks such as maintaining daily to-do lists and using computers, day planners, or calendars to track deadlines and goals; conferring with each other on progress; providing praise when deserved; and making suggestions when appropriate. And you can listen. You can tactfully direct someone to counseling if you have done your research and found a good source of outside help or are aware of an assistance program provided by your employer.

CHAPTER 17

Riding the Roller Coaster of Another Person's Moods

When you find yourself in the company of someone experiencing an episode of mania or depression, your priority should be to keep yourself, others, and the person experiencing the episode safe. Your response will depend on the severity of the episode and may include comforting the individual, arranging a visit to a doctor, or calling for emergency assistance.

When a Loved One Is Manic

Being familiar with the difference between mania and hypomania, as well as bipolar I versus less severe forms of the disorder, can be very helpful if you interact with someone with a mood disorder. In addition to the textbook descriptions of bipolar disorder, it is valuable to learn the symptoms displayed by the individual you want to help.

Hypomanic Episodes

While hypomania, a less extreme version of mania, can escalate to full-scale mania, by itself it rarely poses an emergency situation. You can be reasonably confident that the situation is under control in the following scenarios:

- The person generally responds to treatment. If someone is consistently taking medication and seeing a doctor, she still might become somewhat overstimulated at times. This mood swing might manifest itself as an inability to sit still, stop talking, or concentrate.

- The person is diagnosed as bipolar II, you are familiar with her symptoms, and a doctor has described her normal range of behavior. She might, for example, tend to be driven, highly optimistic, or even slightly grandiose. However, you must keep in mind that cyclothymia, over time, can prog-.ress to bipolar II, which can progress to bipolar I; it is always necessary to watch out for an escalation of mood beyond what the doctor describes as normal for the patient.

- Help is on the way. If you know that the person is about to see a doctor, your only concern may be to confirm that the visit takes place.

It you are uncomfortable with the situation and would prefer not to be around someone acting this way, you are under no obligation to be present. You have every right to excuse yourself.

If you do choose to stay in her company—or if extricating yourself would be difficult—keep in mind that these hypomanic symptoms are beyond her control. If you know her well, have discussed her medical condition with her in the past, and feel comfortable, you can bring the behavior that concerns you to her attention. For example, you could say, "Do you realize you have not stopped talking for fifteen minutes? I think you might need to do something to slow down."

Your words will not end the hypomania. But if her episode is relatively minor, she might be open to trusting you and consult a doctor or do something that in the past has helped to temporarily keep the hypomania under control. It also might be useful to encourage her to join you doing something low key and restful. You might succeed in distracting her from hypomanic thoughts. Should she respond with anger, it could be a sign that symptoms are escalating toward a more serious mania.

Full-Blown Manic and Mixed Episodes

When someone experiences a major manic episode, do what you can to protect all concerned—including yourself. First of all, avoid anything that threatens your finances. Even a seemingly innocuous suggestion that the two of you go to lunch could lead to expenditures beyond your means. You should not let her drive, and you should not rely on her directions to get to an unfamiliar place. If she engages in even minor illegal behavior, you should at the very least disengage yourself. You might also consider this an opportunity to get her help by notifying the police.

 Alert

If you are sexually intimate with a person exhibiting symptoms of full-scale mania, wait until her moods stabilize before having sex. If you are a platonic friend, decline the invitation to join her in any misguided, high-risk sexual adventures.

If she is displaying signs of mania, contact a mental health care professional and other members of her family who could help her get treatment. A serious manic episode can result in very serious problems. Even if in the past she never caused serious harm to herself or others, you must be aware that out-of-control manic behavior can lead to unfortunate events.

A manic episode, or mixed episode with symptoms of depression and agitation, is not something you can make go away by being stern with her, beseeching her to realize what she is doing, or trying to change the subject. They are serious situations which require medical treatment and, in some cases, hospitalization.

Handling a Psychiatric Emergency

First, determine if anyone—patient, relative, or bystander—is in danger. If you feel threatened, get away and call for help. If you sense he might harm himself, call the police or other source of assistance and try to reassure him, if you can do it without risk to yourself. After the threat is removed, be sure he sees a doctor even if he is not hospitalized.

Be Ready to Handle Crises

Experience and education may allow you to learn the warning signs of approaching mood episodes. While some of the indicators may be subtle at first, and difficult to spot, the fact that you are able to focus your attention on the expression of the illness in one individual may allow you to develop considerable skill at predicting the onset of serious symptoms.

Intense mania and manic psychosis can be terrifying for all involved. While waiting for help to arrive, try to reassure and calm him in a low key manner. If possible, do it away from others.

The same advice applies to calling for help. If it is safe for you to make a private call, describe his history and symptoms completely to the mental health professional you contact if she is not familiar with the patient. Try to answer the doctor's questions and follow her advice to call for additional help or take other action, such as leave or call a trusted friend.

Call the police if necessary. Explain to the officers or other emergency responders that the person has bipolar disorder and appears to be having a serious manic episode. They need to know they are dealing with a mentally ill individual and not a criminal reacting to a confrontation. Tell them if you think he is a threat to himself or others, and if he has a weapon of any kind. Make it clear that you are requesting help getting medical treatment for him, that you are not requesting an arrest. Provide them with the name of the patient and his doctor.

In the event of a serious mood episode:

- Always have an escape route clear in your mind.
- Don't stop trying to get help if someone refuses to respond.

- Keep emergency phone numbers—doctor, rescue squad, police—programmed into your phones or listed near phones.
- Don't confront or argue with the patient. Instead, be a reassuring, calming presence.
- Tell the patient who the responders are, that they are there to help, what they will do, and that you will stay with him.

Alert

If someone develops out-of-control manic or even psychotic symptoms, try to stay calm. If a doctor has provided a customized emergency plan for this type of situation, follow the plan's directions. Don't leave the person alone if he might harm himself, providing there is no threat to you. Besides calling a mental health professional, you might also contact someone the patient likes and trusts. Ask this person to talk to the patient.

A person experiencing a severe manic episode may resist attempts to comfort or lead him to professional help. You cannot force someone into a psychiatric hospital without the approval of a doctor. Do not threaten someone with hospitalization or try to force him to a hospital without the assistance and approval of medical or emergency responders.

When a Loved One Is Depressed

Being in the company of a depressed person appears to present completely different challenges than those presented by caring for someone who is manic. Your responsibilities, however, remain the same: to prevent harm from coming to anyone involved and to get medical help for the sufferer. Once you have accomplished these goals, you can direct your attention to comforting the person and encouraging her to participate once again in life.

Minor Situations

If someone is still eating and sleeping, going to work, caring for children, engaging in conversations, and making decisions, the depression may appear to be mild and not life threatening. However, it isn't safe to assume this unless the patient is under a doctor's care. It is essential that a person diagnosed with any form of bipolar disorder receives treatment. The doctor should know that his patient is experiencing a depression that lasts longer than a day or two.

Even if the depression is relatively minor in its severity, such as that associated with cyclothymia, it is far from a pleasant experience for the person who experiences it or for her loved ones. A sense of despondency can permeate the home. Efforts to cheer the person often fail, adding more to the sense of gloom. You might be made to feel as though you are wounding the person just by talking to her.

Again, remember that you did not cause this condition, nor can you make it go away, although you might be able to help her by distracting her from her thoughts and encouraging her to get help. The unhappiness you feel is a normal response to the effects of a chronic disorder affecting someone close to you. It might be helpful to share your feelings with others exposed to the depression.

Essential

People in the midst of a manic or depressive episode may say insulting, dismissive, and hurtful things. Do not take personally what a person in the midst of such a crisis says to you. As difficult as this can be, remember that such behavior is a common feature of the illness.

You should not expect any of these pursuits to make the depression go away. But it is useful in many ways to keep the person from totally isolating herself. Your presence can make a difference.

Major Situations

If the episode has advanced to major depression, she may isolate herself and close down emotionally except for extreme sadness and despair. The person commonly disconnects from others and may take to bed or sit in the dark for hours on end. For her, it can be painful to do anything more; it can hurt just to talk to family members. Expressions of concerns are brushed aside or ignored.

This serious form of depression can lead to a suicide attempt. It is extremely important that she get professional help; you will not be able to snap her out of it. The best thing you can do is to make sure she is seen by a qualified medical professional.

Beyond this, you can let her know that you care, that her presence in your life is important, and that she makes a difference to you and others. You can also try to keep her actively involved in some sort of everyday pursuit. It is not a good idea for her to be completely isolated.

Taking Action versus Distancing Yourself

If someone you care about is manic or depressed, you might feel confused sometimes about when you should try to help and when you should instead take care of your own needs. There are no absolute rules, but there are some general guidelines.

When to Speak Up

Although there is nothing you can do to cure someone's bipolar disorder and the episodes that characterize it, you can monitor the situation, be available when needed, and summon help when necessary. Some situations where you might be able to help are when:

- **The person has stopped taking medication.** There are legal options available to order the person back into treatment, as previously discussed. You can call his doctor to ask for advice. If appropriate for you personally, you can tell him that you cannot continue the relationship as usual unless he resumes treatment. Depending on the nature of your relationship, you can refuse to live under the same roof or see each other socially, until he has resumed treatment.

- **The medical help seems incompetent or inadequate.** If you find out, for example, that his regular psychiatrist is out of town for two weeks and did not leave any sort of referral, or you call to say your loved one is severely depressed or suicidal and the doctor does not seem particularly concerned, help him find additional help and a new doctor. You can also take your loved one to a hospital yourself, if he is willing to go with you.

- **A manic person is about to do something dangerous or destructive.** In the throes of arrogant mania, someone might feel indestructible. If you can safely stop him from doing something dangerous or illegal, do so. You can also try to get him to a hospital or doctor's office—even if it means deceiving him. If he is unwilling to accompany you, you can call the police if he appears to be a threat to himself or others.

- **A depressed person seems to be on the verge of suicide.** If you cannot take legal steps to get the person into treatment, do what you have to do to get him to a doctor or hospital. You might try by honestly saying you are taking him where help can be provided. But if the suicidal impulse is strong, you are likely to be met with powerful resistance. If you are convinced he is seriously contemplating suicide, contact his doctor or another qualified mental health professional and follow her advice. You can also call 1-800-273-TALK (8255) or 1-1-800-SUICIDE (784-2433). If necessary, call the police for assistance in saving his life.

When to Distance Yourself

People with bipolar disorder, like anyone else, appreciate knowing there are people who care about them. They may not be particularly conscious of it during a serious mood episode, but they care. The help they receive can make a great deal of difference in their lives. Still, there are situations in which it might be appropriate to distance yourself from him and leave him in the care of someone else.

L. Essential

If you provide emotional support for someone with bipolar disorder, you will be more effective if you learn about the disorder and the way it affects the person you care for. Familiarity with the particular form of the illness that affects your loved one can improve your ability to manage the disorder and deal with setbacks. It can also help you cope with the challenge of caring for someone overcoming a mental disorder. Increase your knowledge with family therapy, books, and support groups.

When he is responding well to treatment and has a good network of personal and professional support, you should not feel as though you have to stay actively involved in his problems unless there is a close attachment. People with bipolar disorder—like everyone else—need to respect other people's preferences and wishes. If you have other things you want or need to do that don't involve someone whose treatment is working, you are under no obligation to sacrifice your needs just because your friend has a disorder.

When someone needs a lot of help and support and you are impatient, it might seem easier to solve all his problems by yourself. Sometimes it is hard to know when to stop getting involved. The goal of treatment is to have someone reach a point where they can do as much for themselves as they can. With the guidance of a doctor or therapist, you will be able to figure out how much someone can handle with and without your help. As long as someone is learning from minor mistakes, you are not shirking your responsibility if you let them work through the process.

 Fact

If you feel endangered by a spouse, ex-spouse, or person you dated, consider filing an Order for Protection (OFP). An OFP will define the restrictions on contact the other party must obey, as well as the terms of custody and child support, restitution, mandatory counseling, and property and money issues, as applicable. An alternative to an OFP is a Harassment Restraining Order (HRO), which does not require having lived with or dated the harassing party.

If you honestly feel as though you cannot help the person anymore, you cannot stand to be interrupted anymore, and that your own well-being is threatened by your association with someone with bipolar disorder, your best options might be to arrange other help for him and extricate yourself. If you merely pity someone, your underlying scorn is likely to reveal itself, and you are doing neither yourself nor him any favors by pretending to care.

Dealing with Caregiver Stress

Caring for someone with a serious mental disorder can be very difficult. Two-thirds of caregivers cannot find enough time for themselves, according to a survey by the National Alliance on Mental Illness.

Besides the stress inherent in dealing with extreme mood fluctuations, caregivers may face frustration from dealing with chores that accompany a serious illness revolving around insurance companies, doctors' appointments, and varieties of red tape.

The Stress

Caregiver stress appears to increase with the severity of the illness. Watch for indications of depression, irritability, anxiety, frustration, anger, fatigue, insomnia or other sleep disturbances, and difficulty concentrating. Another sign you have taken on too much is poor physical health due to a weakened immune system and exhaustion.

When you are troubled by any of the above signs, look for help in the form of assistance from friends or family, from psychoeducational programs, support groups, or from a personal therapist.

If there is any way you can arrange it, schedule some time away from your caregiver responsibilities. Make the most of any time you can get away. Even brief periods of getting outdoors, exercising, or socializing can have a significant positive effect. Don't allow your life to be completely consumed by bipolar disorder.

Essential

The symptoms of bipolar disease can be very trying. They can frighten and demoralize you, and cause you to lose patience. It can help if you consciously strive to separate the healthy personality of the person you care for from the symptoms of the illness. This can allow you to maintain an emotional distance from the disease while continuing to appreciate the person affected by it.

Feeling there is no escape is often an important element of stress. If you become convinced there is no way out of your present situation, you may conclude your only option is to give up or press on until you no longer can. To avoid reaching this extreme state, you need to have control of some part of your personal life.

You have a good chance of reducing your stress levels if you can manage to get good rest and nutrition, exercise, laughter, and relaxation. To achieve these elusive goals, a caregiver must separate herself in some way for some time from her responsibilities.

Your Protection

If you live with someone whose treatment is ineffective—especially one who has a history of violent behavior—you should safeguard your environment. Even if you do not live together, if the person is a close relative or best friend who stops over frequently, you might want to do the following:

- **Keep drugs and alcohol out of reach.** Except for his medications and over-the-counter products you know do not negatively interact with treatment, keep your own prescription drugs hidden or locked away.
- **Keep weapons locked up.** This is obvious, but a person prone to violent episodes should not have access to a gun. If you feel you must have a gun in the house, keep it hidden and locked. Store ammunition separately. You also would be wise to keep kitchen and other knives similarly hidden.
- **Have a safe space.** There should be a room in the house equipped with a strong door and lock, where you can hide safely.
- **Do not live under the same roof.** If a loved one assaults you, do not let him move back in. If you must see the person, limit your contacts to public settings, with other people around to serve as witnesses.

If the person is starting to behave in a potentially violent manner, the first thing you should do is call the police. You should have the emergency numbers entered into your cell phone for instant, one-touch dialing. If you have police emergency reports in the house, you can fill them out in advance, so that the police can act quickly when they arrive. Include information about the person's diagnosis and doctor.

After a Serious Episode

Caring for yourself is no less important than caring for someone with bipolar disorder. If a relapse has resulted in your loved one being hospitalized, he is receiving the care he needs. It then becomes your responsibility to make sure you get the care you need.

If the incident has been particularly upsetting, it means you have experienced an emotional trauma. If you have reactions such as sleep disturbance, nightmares, problems concentrating, or a desire to isolate yourself for days after the crisis, discuss it with someone you trust—a therapist, social worker, friend, or family. Don't try to forget about it. Such feelings take much less of a toll on you psychologically if you deal with them openly.

Your Options

Ultimately, it is up to the person with bipolar disorder to take responsibility to find the best treatment and to stick to it. It is also up to her to seek therapy, eat and sleep well, stay away from recreational drugs, and follow a lifestyle that minimizes the likelihood of having a mood episode. You cannot control another person; you cannot make her get better or guarantee she follows a treatment plan. You can provide a loving and supportive presence. You can have fun together and explore life together, whether as intimate partners, friends, or relatives. Your presence does not determine everything, but it can have a positive effect.

While there are quite a few things you can do to help someone with this disorder, there are also a number of things you cannot do for her.

It's very important to remember these boundaries for your own safety and peace of mind.

- You cannot make the disorder go away. You did not cause it, and you cannot cure it.

- You cannot fully predict if or when an episode will start or end. You can gain considerable insight into her behavioral patterns, but you cannot know for certain what will trigger an episode or how long it will last.
- You cannot make an episode go away. Talking to her reasonably or humoring her will not make the symptoms stop.
- You cannot make someone having a full-blown manic episode calm down. Mania goes beyond your ability to be a calming influence.
- You cannot make someone having a major depressive episode become cheerful.
- You cannot control whether or not someone decides to go off medication. You can work with professionals and the court system to try to get the person back on medication.

You Don't Have to Be a Caregiver

If someone you love has bipolar disorder, you will probably want to do all you can to help her. The extent of your responsibilities will depend on the severity of the symptoms. Someone whose bipolar symptoms are under control doesn't need a caregiver unless a serious relapse occurs. As long as a treatment plan is followed, a caregiver's responsibilities are minimal. But someone who suffers from bipolar I, say, and is subject to frequent relapses will need much more attention.

If the situation becomes more than you can handle, discuss it with her doctor, social worker, and/or therapist. Tell them you can no longer provide effective care. Ask them for advice on how you can find help. If alcohol or illegal drug use by the patient is a factor, as it often is, alert mental health care providers and seek ways to direct her to a drug rehabilitation program.

It's Understandable If You Cannot Be a Caregiver

Not everyone can handle high or even moderate amounts of stress on a daily basis. Different people have different capacities.

It is your right to decline or limit your contact with someone who makes your life unbearably difficult. Obviously, if the person is a threat to herself or others, you have an obligation to tell authorities who can handle the situation, but there is no law that says you have to allow someone else, even someone you love who has a mental illness, to create chaos in your life. You won't be a good caregiver if you feel the disruption to your life is so great you are not sure if you can cope.

There is still, unfortunately, a shortage of qualified mental health care workers and options for treating difficult cases in the United States. It won't always be easy to find someone to step in for you when you feel overwhelmed. That is why it is so important to learn all about the mental health services, programs, and resources available in your community.

CHAPTER 18

Ongoing Controversies

The causes of many diseases are complex and remain unidentified. Furthermore, patients have individual differences that prevent a cookie-cutter approach to treatment. Modern medicine is moving toward becoming a science, but it still requires a bit of applied art. This situation, not surprisingly, leads some people to question the value of fields like psychiatry. For the majority of patients, experience has shown over and over that properly prescribed and used psychotropic medications, combined with education and therapy, go a long way to lessening, and in many cases controlling, the symptoms of mental disorders. Nevertheless, a minority of people remain vocal critics of current practice.

How Can You Classify Mood Disorders?

Mood disorders considered by themselves are complicated enough: the general category includes three major subdivisions (bipolar, depressive, and schizoaffective), each divided into three subdivisions for diagnostic purposes. When you consider the range of normal moods that border on the highs and lows associated with these disorders, the degree of complexity expands many times. Sorting out where one ends and another begins assumes that they are distinct from each other, an assumption that makes labeling easy but understanding less so. The suffix NOS, not otherwise specified, is added to some diagnoses of mood disorders to describe patterns of illness that don't fit into the other categories. Moods and their disorders in humans appear not to be distinct states, but part of a rich spectrum. The subdivisions and labels change as we learn more about them. It is safe to regard them as temporary, subject to reclassification in response to new research.

Bipolar Moods and Normal Moods

Some people believe there are more varieties of bipolar disorder than bipolar I, II, and cyclothymia. If people with consistent signs of hypomania, for example, were included in the category, then the prevalence rate of bipolar disorder might double.

Are There Other, Mild Forms of Bipolar Disorder?

Some people would include in the category a consistently elevated mood called hyperthymia. Being constantly upbeat and always enthusiastic is not unheard of, but it is not the norm in the general population. It is more common to experience a fairly steady, neither-too-high-nor-too-low mood characterized by some contentment, some discontentment, some happiness, and some sadness—usually associated with external events such as receiving good news, problems with personal relationships, etc. However, other people, including many doctors, are skeptical about attempts to, as one put it, "see bipolar disorder everywhere."

Does a long-lasting, exuberant mood that causes no problem need to be placed on the spectrum of mood disorders? In a clinical sense, no. If it poses no threat to anyone's health, it is not a concern for psychiatrists. Cataloging and understanding a mental state like this, however, may help us better understand the full spectrum of emotional states related to mood disorders and provide clues about what can go wrong when moods become extreme.

Hyperthymia

Some people always seem to be upbeat and energetic, trying new things and initiating new projects. This trait, which is sometimes called hyperthymia, is not unlike being on a "permanent high." Some people argue that hyperthymia is a type of mood disorder that results in high activity and inflated sense of self-esteem— something like living with constant hypomania but with the crucial difference that it is not as clearly episodic. Instead, it seems to last and is without any associated depression.

While observations of many people indicate some of them have this mood trait, hyperthymic disorder is not recognized as a mood disorder by either of the two mainstream authorities, the American Psychiatric Association and the World Health Organization. It appears in neither of their diagnostic manuals, the DSM IV and the ICD-10.

On the surface, people with hyperthymia seem optimistic and full of energy. They radiate self-confidence and self-reliance; they seem to believe they can do whatever needs to be done. They thrive on new experiences that promise variety, intrigue, and novelty. Usually, they have a great many personal interests, as well as plans for the future. They also can be articulate and witty.

It might be most accurate to think of hyperthymia as a temperament or personality trait rather than as a marker of a mental disorder. Of course, if this trait causes problems, then it becomes a legitimate subject for psychological or psychiatric care.

In fact, criticism of mainstream psychiatry is often directed at its alleged predisposition to label people with problems that don't exist. The inclusion of homosexuality in earlier editions of the DSM IV—an error since corrected—is a frequently cited example. The reality is if someone is not unhappy, suffering, or a threat to themselves or others, psychiatrists have no reason to intervene. They are busy enough treating people with serious mental problems. It is only when complaints or serious problems appear that the labels of the DSM IV are applied as part of the process for providing effective treatment. A hyperthymic personality can be satisfying, productive, and creative. But if for some individuals it is a manifestation of a part of a spectrum of mood disorders, it could be problematic. For example, some people later diagnosed with bipolar disorder first seek help with depression after they have experienced a setback in their lives. A close look back over their lives may reveal that they have been hyperthymic. Rather than having easily recognizable mood swings, these people may have been experiencing years of constant emotional elevation and enthusiasm along with a long history of uncompleted endeavors.

Also, the lack of a healthy response to the full range of life experience might cause problems for some people who always seem to have elevated spirits. A full, healthy life for most people includes periods of elation and introspection, action and reflection. If only one pole of our emotional lives is present, we may miss the benefits of the counterbalancing half of our responses to events. Consequently, we may lack understanding and empathy in the way we interact with people and respond to events in our lives.

Bipolar Disorder and Schizophrenia

The overlap of symptoms in several types of mental disorders can make it difficult to make a diagnosis with confidence. This can happen, for example, with bipolar disorder and depression, and with bipolar disorder and schizophrenia. Modern psychiatry, in fact, recognizes a mood disorder called schizoaffective bipolar disorder, which has symptoms common to both illnesses.

It's not known if schizophrenia and bipolar disorder lie on the same spectrum or if they lie on intersecting spectrums of separate diseases. It is known that both have been linked to genes located on the same chromosomes. Both are associated with similar, if not always identical, structural abnormalities in the brain. Antipsychotic medication is an effective treatment for many patients suffering from either disease. And the incident rates of both illnesses are affected by season of birth, with increases in the spring and winter.

Having a relative with either disorder is associated with increased risk of having a similar disorder. So, a family history of schizophrenia is associated with an increased risk of bipolar disorder, for example. All of these facts are consistent with a link between the two disorders, but don't prove such a link.

Other facts argue against a strong association. For example, women tend to develop schizophrenia later and have less severe symptoms than men, yet bipolar disorder affects women and men equally. Cognitive problems are more commonly seen in schizophrenia. This is probably one reason that few people with schizophrenia are able to excel in creative fields, whereas many people with bipolar disorder have artistic accomplishments. Lithium is remarkably successful in the treatment of bipolar disorder but not schizophrenia. When medications don't work for bipolar disorder, electroconvulsive therapy often does. This is not true for schizophrenia.

Unfortunately, we still don't know enough about the brain and how it malfunctions to sort out the cause of different mental disorders.

Anti-Medication/Anti-Psychiatry

It is commonly known that sometimes people's attitudes toward medication or the psychiatric community become obstacles toward receiving treatment. These sentiments also play out in a larger arena of public debate.

Anti-Medication

Some people who have never experienced hallucinations, psychosis, or serious mood swings believe that medication is an artificial way of dealing with what are nothing more than personal psychological issues. If people with mental illnesses would simply come to terms with their childhood or change jobs or stop whining, these critics argue, then they would not need medication.

Other critics of modern medicine and psychiatry are devoted to a natural diet and lifestyle. They believe there is a natural remedy, often involving diet, exercise, vitamins, or herbs, for most or all health problems. These views, unfortunately, are not supported by evidence and perpetuate misunderstanding about mental illness.

Fact

Actor and Scientologist Tom Cruise said in 2005, "...with psychiatry, there is no science behind it. And to pretend that there is a science behind it is criminal." Facts: The ability of antipsychotic drugs to control psychotic symptoms is strongly correlated to their ability to bind to specific receptors in the brain. Brain-imaging studies show abnormalities associated with schizophrenia and bipolar disorder. Genetic links to mental disorders have been demonstrated by multiple researchers all over the world. Standard therapy for multiple psychiatric disorders has been proven to reduce hospitalizations and relapses.

Extremists declare that medication should never be used in the treatment of mental disorders. The Internet, for example, has many personal web pages where the owner takes a strong anti-medication stance. Some organized groups, Scientologists for example, condemn psychiatric treatment, claiming that treatment lies not in the hands of modern medicine but in the treatments Scientology offer.

TABLE 18-1: MYTHS AND FACTS ABOUT PSYCHIATRIC MEDICATIONS

Myth	Fact
They are addictive.	They are not habit forming.
They make users "high."	They do not produce euphoria. (Antidepressants inappropriately prescribed for bipolar disorder, however, can relieve depression and allow mania to emerge in some patients).

TABLE 18-1: MYTHS AND FACTS ABOUT PSYCHIATRIC MEDICATIONS (continued)

Myth	Fact
They control peoples' minds.	Appropriate medications at the right doses do not act as "chemical straightjackets."
They are "knock-out" drugs.	Some can have sedating effects, but their value is in diminishing psychotic and other extreme symptoms.
They take away "free will."	They help patients overcome debilitating symptoms so they can deal with problems rationally. Many people with bipolar disorder claim they can work more productively and creatively because of their medication.

Sources: Adapted from New York State Office of Mental Health and National Institute of Mental Health

Are Nontraditional Treatments Better Than Standard Treatments?

Alternative or nontraditional treatments include different types of therapies and healing philosophies. They might work for some complaints, but there is no proof they work better than mainstream medical treatment for bipolar or other serious mental disorders.

Nearly all medical scientists agree that people with psychiatric disorders should not rely on alternative treatments to the exclusion of established therapies. If, however, they present no health threats and don't interfere with effective treatments, some alternative therapies might be helpful, particularly if they make someone feel more relaxed. Just be sure to tell your doctor, pharmacist, etc., about all the treatments you are using or techniques you are practicing.

Anti-Psychiatry

Psychiatry also has critics who believe that mental illness is a sham invented to control people and make money for doctors. Or they think that some people like having a mental diagnosis because it gets them attention or serves as an excuse for their behavior and problems.

Other people cannot see beyond their own life experience. Since they have never lost control of their emotions, no one else should. And if someone does claim to have a mental problem, they must be faking it or they are just weak. Since the critic has survived difficult challenges, he is unsympathetic to anyone else who appears to need help.

Many of the same groups that oppose medication also oppose psychiatry and for many of the same reasons. But opponents of these groups counter that psychiatrists and psychologists are, in effect, in direct competition with these religious and cult groups. People often join these groups because they feel something missing in their lives, and they are often required to give time and money to the group. If they were to give time and money to a psychiatrist, the group would lose out. Rather than having someone see a credentialed and licensed professional health care provider, some groups want people to see their own healers and remain under the group's influence.

Good Pharmaceutical Industry or Bad Drug Companies?

Other critics abhor the profit motivation of the pharmaceutical industry. They believe that all the industry cares about is making money, and that it will promote and even invent disorders in order to produce a drug to treat them.

Pharmaceutical companies are competitive businesses that want to maximize profits. But it is also true that it can take decades to get a single new drug approved by the FDA, and that millions of dollars have gone into the research to develop it. Yet whether corporate greed outweighs altruistic motives or not, criticisms launched at pharmaceutical companies can lead some people to conclude that they should not trust—or take—medications that have been demonstrated in controlled tests to work for a significant number of people.

Even many critics of the field of psychiatry admit that many mental illnesses respond to psychopharmacology, the treatment of mental disorders with medications. But, they add, the makers of those medications overpromote their use by overpromoting their need—all for more profits. Psychiatrists, the critics claim, play into the hands of the industry by recognizing more mental disorders.

Defenders counter by saying that psychiatry is learning more about the relationships of different disorders and describing them in more detail, just what you would expect from an advancing field of medical research.

Do Pharmaceutical Companies Have Too Much Influence?

Most pharmaceutical companies try to influence psychiatrists to prescribe their medications; that is how they make a profit. A good psychiatrist, of course, wouldn't prescribe a medication in response to this pressure. Sometimes, people can't be sure how much doctors are influenced if the doctors accept money to act as consultants to drug companies. Some mental health advocacy groups such as The National Alliance on Mental Illness, National Mental Health Association, and the Bazelon Center for Mental Health for example, have accepted funding from pharmaceutical companies in the past. Even the American Psychiatric Association has accepted funds from the industry. These organizations provide excellent services to the public and should be respected for providing and promoting information about mental health. There is, however, an appearance of conflict of interest if an advocacy or professional group does not warn the public that it accepts money from a pharmaceutical manufacturer.

Short of not taking money from the pharmaceutical industry, the best solution to this problem is for all doctors and organizations to publically disclose from whom they accept money and for what purpose. This allows patients to make up their own minds and satisfies their right to know about potential conflicts of interest.

Privacy Issues

The U.S. Supreme Court has affirmed your right to keep your medical records private. This right is necessary so patients will not hesitate to tell their doctors all relevant information. The law is also designed to protect people from experiencing discrimination in their private lives in areas such as employment, housing, and personal finance.

Confidentiality

Unfortunately, stigma surrounding mental illness can result in great damage if someone's private medical history is not protected: lost jobs, lost promotions, denied housing, etc.

If you are concerned about your privacy, ask your health care providers how they protect your confidentiality. Ask exactly what they disclose to insurance companies and others if they share vital information.

 Alert

If someone such as a prospective employer, an insurer, or a government agency requests information about you from your doctor, it is supposed to be released only if you sign an authorization form. The American Psychiatric Association Guidelines on Confidentiality state "the patient's consent to the release of information from his or her medical record should be informed and given freely, without threat or coercion."

A psychiatrist can be forced to release medical records without a patient's consent if a court orders it. In this event, it is the responsibility of the doctor to release only enough material to satisfy the legal requirements of the order, and no more.

A subpoena, a demand to appear in court and testify, is not the same thing as a court order, and a psychiatrist cannot reveal a patient's private medical history in response to it, unless the patient agrees. The only other time a doctor can release private medical information is if she is convinced a patient might physically harm someone. Then she is required by law to report the perceived threat to the police.

Forced Treatment

A serious controversy surrounding medical record privacy involves attempts by third parties, who could benefit from knowing a patient's medical history, to obtain the records. A bit more controversy surrounds the question: Should someone ever be forced to receive treatment?

For some people, the answer is clearly no, because a principle is at stake: the right of an individual to make her own decisions. Even when there seem to be compelling reasons to force someone into treatment, a question lingers for these critics: Who will be next? And what if a person does not respond to treatment? Is it in someone's interest to be forced to have ineffective treatment?

Essential

In January 1999, a man who had schizophrenia but was not taking medication pushed a woman into the path of subway train in New York City. This tragedy led to a law in New York State enabling courts to order outpatients to receive treatment when community safety seems at risk.

Most people support the legal justifications that allow authorities to make medication a condition of parole or release. Moreover, most people agree that mental disorders frequently render patients incapable of understanding their need for help and that their behavior may necessitate intervention for their own good and for the good of others.

The Treatment Advocacy Center (TAC) endorses this position, and advocates changing state laws so that people who are unaware of the seriousness of their mental illness can receive the benefits of treatment. You can learn more at: *www.psychlaws.org*. TAC notes, "It is the illness, not the treatment that restricts civil liberties." People who support this approach agree that patients who have been freed of psychotic thoughts and uncontrollable mood swings are in a better position to defend their civil liberties than people incapacitated by the symptoms of severe bipolar and other mental disorders.

No Other Choice

For most people, hospitalization is an acceptable and perhaps the only choice when symptoms become so severe they cannot benefit from outpatient care or when a person is in the midst of a psychiatric emergency.

 Fact

You can consult with a lawyer, social worker, or health care provider about starting the legal process to enforce treatment if you care for someone who refuses to take medication. They can tell you how to arrange a psychiatric evaluation. With their advice, you can approach a court with an Emergency Petition if you are concerned that someone poses a threat to herself or others.

The National Alliance for the Mentally Ill estimates that nearly 90 percent of patients in psychiatric hospitals agreed to be admitted. The rest first had to be certified by a physician as needing hospitalization. The criteria for deciding someone should be involuntarily hospitalized vary by state. Nowhere is it easy to have someone committed and forced to undergo treatment. The laws protecting people against involuntary hospitalization are strict.

Involuntary Hospital Admissions

If a doctor decides to admit a patient into a hospital without her permission, in most cases the confinement is limited to a few weeks or less. In every case, a judge should be informed of an involuntary commitment and the legal rights of the patient should be protected before, during, and after the period of confinement.

If the psychiatric evaluation indicates a need for further treatment in the hospital, the stay can be extended following a court hearing at which the patient, legal guardian, or someone approved by the court to represent the patient is present.

In many cases, treatment results in enough improvement that the patient can soon be released for outpatient therapy. Anytime doctors recommend long-term commitment, they have to convince a court it is necessary.

If there is any way a patient can be effectively treated without full-time commitment, for example, part-time hospitalization, residential care, or supervised independent living, that option should be chosen, providing it can provide effective treatment.

The Insanity Defense

As anyone who watches TV crime shows knows, the insanity defense argues that a defendant cannot be held accountable for a crime if his mental illness made it impossible for him to distinguish right from wrong when he committed the crime. The heinous nature of many violent and sexual crimes causes many people to find this defense repugnant. However, others argue that it is a necessary component of the justice system.

Arguments in Support of the Insanity Defense

Many legal, medical, and ethics professionals are convinced that when someone is mentally ill, it is unjust to hold the defendant accountable for her actions; it is wrong to punish someone who had no control over her actions.

It is more humane, they insist, that a ruling of not guilty by reason of insanity allows a patient to be committed to a psychiatric treatment facility. There, the patient can be held safely away from the public and receive treatment. Illnesses require treatment in a civilized society. Punishing someone who is ill is unjustifiable, no matter how horrible her crimes.

Arguments Against the Insanity Defense

Other people believe that justice means people always have to pay for what they have done. This view assumes that even if someone is mentally ill, she can still understand the difference between right and wrong.

Quite often, the meticulous way in which the crime was committed and the painstaking steps the defendant took not to get caught makes it more difficult to convince a jury the defendant did not know what she was doing. In fact, attempts to hide or cover up a crime can undermine the defense in the eyes of a jury.

Furthermore, some people find it unjust not to punish someone for committing a violent act. Many victims and their families are unlikely to feel that justice has been served otherwise.

 Fact

The insanity defense is used in only about 1 percent of criminal cases, and is successful only about 25 percent of the time. In about 80 percent of these instances, it is because a plea bargain has been worked out in advance with the prosecution.

These controversies, and others, will continue as long as there is more to be learned about mental illness. That process depends on society's attitude toward mental illness, the success of efforts to increase public knowledge and reduce stigma, and the amount of money spent to research the basic causes and find new treatments for diseases like bipolar disorder.

CHAPTER 19

Where Do You Go from Here?

In this book, a great many issues surrounding bipolar disorder have been discussed, including its different forms, its causes, the importance of treatment, and how it affects people's lives. Now, as you prepare for your future, there are a few more ideas to keep in mind. Whether you have bipolar disorder or are close to someone who does, remember that the diagnosis means you have an excellent chance of controlling your moods and your life. With effective treatment, you will be free to work to accomplish the goals you choose and have healthy relationships with other people.

Summary

If you can remember just two things from this book, remember that bipolar disorder is an extremely serious, but largely treatable, diagnosis. It therefore does not have to rule or ruin your life and the lives of those close to you.

Bipolar Disorder Is Serious

To receive an accurate diagnosis of bipolar disorder is to receive one of the most serious diagnoses in the field of psychiatry. If you ignore it, if your symptoms remain untreated, you could end up in a prison, a psychiatric hospital, or in a situation that increases your risk of suicide. You could easily find yourself broke and in debt, jobless with little chance of future employment, and isolated from other people because you cannot sustain healthy relationships.

This pessimistic prediction stems from the fact that untreated bipolar disorder goes way beyond the normal shifts of mood experienced by most people. In an episode of mania, you might commit acts of violence against other people, destroy property, lose money, acquire sexually transmitted diseases through unsafe sex, and frighten and alienate the people you care about.

If you do not have bipolar disorder but are close to someone who does—and this person is not receiving treatment—you might feel as if you are at the mercy of his moods. It might be hard to plan ahead because you never know when a major mood swing will cause everything to change for the worse.

Even if you neither have the disorder nor know someone who does, you are still affected by it in terms of your tax dollar and by the loss of productivity to the nation and world. Bipolar disorder is not a passing phase in someone's life. It will not go away through wishful thinking, positive thinking, yelling and screaming, or by being extra nice.

Bipolar Disorder Is Treatable

Medication—usually a combination of pharmaceutical compounds—can keep the various symptoms under control. These medications can include mood stabilizers, anti-depressants, anti-psychotics, anti-anxiety drugs, and sleep aids. A large number of patients find a highly effective regime of treatment. For others, medication is partially effective. A minority of patients do not respond to medication or cannot take it because of side effects.

Medication, although not 100 percent effective, has on balance made an enormous difference for people with this mood disorder. Moreover, no other treatments have proven to be nearly as effective as those currently prescribed by psychiatrists to treat bipolar disorder.

Perhaps most important of all, you might see a therapist to improve your human relations skills. This step, as well as taking care of yourself by eating well, exercising, maintaining a stable home or apartment, and having healthy relationships, is important for maintaining your health. A positive environment that minimizes stress and avoidance of alcohol and street drugs will lesson the chances of experiencing severe mood swings. None of these important steps, however, will treat the underlying biological cause of your symptoms; only medication will do this. However, the effectiveness of the medication will be increased by adding appropriate therapy and avoiding drugs and alcohol. Perhaps at some point in the future there will be an alternate treatment just as effective, or even a cure, but at present, medication is as good as it gets. Compared to what was available fifty or even twenty years ago, treatment today represents a significant advance.

Staying on medication can be a major challenge for many people. The nature of the illness itself makes it difficult for some people to recognize how ill they are. Even after wild mood swings are stabilized for a time, some people tire of having to take medication. Having an episode can mistakenly start to seem no worse than dealing with adverse side effects or the monotony of routine treatment. Again, this type of reasoning can often be traced to the effect of mood swings on a person's critical and reasoning ability.

Steer Clear of Excuses

Just in case there are lingering doubts about the validity of bipolar disorder as a diagnosable and treatable condition, here are some remaining myths, misconceptions, and excuses sometimes offered to convince someone that the symptoms are not related to a serious mental illness. For example, someone may suggest that something currently happening in your life is being mistaken for bipolar disorder:

- **"Just being dramatic."** You or the other person simply like to overdramatize how good or bad everything is. He should probably just take an acting class to get it out of his system.

- **"Just a vivid imagination."** Similarly, you merely like to make things seem more intriguing or complex than they are. All you need to do is take a writing or drawing class in order to express your heightened perceptions.
- **"Just craving attention."** You demand a great deal of attention from other people, and only know how to get it by acting out. You simply need to learn more constructive ways of asking for help, reassurance, or company.
- **"Just been working too hard."** You get upset or anger easily, have trouble slowing down, or don't get out of bed because of work pressure and career demands.
- **"Just not working enough."** The problem is that you have been out of work or don't have enough to do or think about. No wonder you are making such a fuss.
- **"Just upset about other things."** Highly erratic and unpredictable behavior is the result of day-to-day pressures or problems. You don't have bipolar disorder; you've just been recently divorced, involved in a legal dispute, given birth, or been fired. No wonder you're having some problems adjusting.

Other excuses suggest a more long-term problem or blame something in your past:

- **"Just an unhappy childhood."** The disturbing behavior is not really due to a mood disorder; it's just the kind of acting out you would expect from someone who suffered serious childhood traumas. (Of course, while it is true that past trauma can exacerbate bipolar symptoms, it does not mean there are no bipolar symptoms).
- **"Just alcohol or drug issues."** (Again, this is tricky, as alcohol or drug abuse can also make inherent bipolar symptoms worse. But while it is possible for someone to be an alcoholic or drug addict and not have bipolar disorder, it is also

possible to be an addict and/or alcoholic with bipolar disorder. In fact, nearly half of people with this mood disorder have problems with substance abuse at some point.)

- **"Everyone is this way sometimes."** Everyone has their ups and downs, their good and bad days, and everyone feels highly stressed sometimes. Therefore, there is no reason for alarm. (Mood swings with bipolar disorder are extreme and anything but normal.)

- **"The person functions, so there's no real problem."** Since you manage to work, go to school, and/or raise children, you can't have a serious mental disorder. (This objection does not consider the efficiency with which these tasks are carried out or the damage that is done during bipolar episodes.)

- **"Just making excuses for yourself."** Claiming to have a mood disorder is an easy way out of taking responsibility for past actions and present failures. (Bipolar disorder is a legitimate mental disorder recognized by modern medicine and diagnosed according to strict criteria.)

- **"Just the latest excuse."** You are claiming to have a disorder that has been in the news and is associated with celebrities and accomplished, famous people of the past. (This, however, doesn't mean that someone with extreme mood fluctuations is adopting the diagnosis to be trendy. Depending on her medical symptoms and history, she indeed may have the disorder.)

Bipolar Disorder and the Future

Despite the advances in the treatment of bipolar disorder in recent decades, there are many areas where we hope and expect to see new research translate eventually into better understanding of the disorder and more effective treatment. Obviously, the identification of specific genes and combinations of genes related to the development and onset of bipolar disorder promises to increase significantly our understanding of this illness and suggest new therapeutic targets. While this avenue of research is often discussed, other approaches may turn out to be just as promising.

Imaging the Brain

Today, it is possible to see deep inside the brain of a living person. The equipment may be bulky, but the images they produce are impressive and informative. When brain-imaging tools (such as functional magnetic resonance imaging and positron emission tomography) are directed at the brains of people with bipolar disorder, we get to look at the organ where mood disorders originate and go out of control.

So far, we have learned there may be a common pattern of brain development in some people that makes them susceptible to mood disorders. Other neuroimaging studies have found specific brain regions that are larger or smaller than normal in the brains of people with bipolar disorder. Continued research along these lines, combined with information gained from genetic studies, should help scientists better understand psychiatric illnesses. When we better understand the brain in health and disease, scientists may someday be able to develop better treatments and predict which types of treatment will work most effectively in an individual. All patients, and especially those now resistant to treatment, might benefit from the development of new drugs and better understanding of the underlying basis of the disorder.

Far in the future, it may even be possible to head off the development of illnesses like bipolar disorder. But that won't happen until billions of dollars have been invested in mental health research.

Better Insight into Mood

It isn't easy to convince someone experiencing a manic episode to cooperate with a researcher and lie perfectly still while images of his brain are made. It is much easier to obtain the cooperation of someone who is experiencing hyperthymia or perhaps hypomania, less-than-manic but still elevated moods. Perhaps, better understanding of mood changes such as these will be helpful in understanding more serious mood fluctuations.

It may be useful, for example, to investigate the nature of subthreshold moods; that is, mental states that don't quite satisfy the criteria for mood disorders set out by the American Psychiatric Association—bipolar I, II, and cyclothymia as well as depressive disorders. Some researchers believe that clinically significant subthreshold bipolar disorder may be as common as what is now recognized as biopolar disorder. What we learn about the spectrum of mood disorders may advance our understanding of the most serious forms such as major depression and bipolar I.

Slowly Diminishing Stigma?

Stigma has long been and remains a challenge for people with mental disorders and their families.

Advocacy groups are making progress in fighting back the ignorance that fuels misconceptions surrounding psychiatric care. Some politicians are becoming more aware of the problem, too. They showed it by passing a bill that requires businesses with fifty or more employees to provide equal insurance coverage for physical and mental health problems. The bill, which went into effect at the start of 2010, followed ten years of lobbying by mental health care advocates. It will correct injustices such as higher deductibles, higher copayments, and limited treatment options for people being treated for addiction and mental illness.

Another positive development is the publicity that bipolar and other mental disorders receive when celebrities discuss their experiences with it or become advocates and fundraisers for organizations that promote better understanding. Popular culture in the U.S. is largely driven by celebrities, and their activities can have a significant impact on how all kinds of illnesses are perceived. Continuation of this trend would be a positive way to educate the public in a society that devotes large amounts of time and money to celebrity watching. Increasing public awareness could lead to better allocation of funds for research by the federal government. At the very least, it may result in increased familiarity with mental disorders and less stigma.

Essential

Despite the dismal statistics on suicide, crime, cost to the taxpayer, and cost to the economy, bipolar disorder and other serious mental conditions traditionally have not attracted the same interest or sympathy on the part of the general public as other illnesses that afflict far fewer people. A good example is suicide, a serious risk in mood disorders. It's seldom discussed, although it ranks among the major causes of death in the U.S. and around the world.

Emma Parker Bowles dealt with bipolar disorder for years. She found that "admitting I have a mental illness is the first step in the road to recovery. Sharing it takes the power out of it. To hell with you, bipolar. I am not ashamed any more."

Finding Role Models

You don't need to have bipolar disorder to benefit from finding positive role models, people who set a good example for you to follow. They don't have to be great or famous men and women, although they can be. They might be found among people you encounter every day, if you look for them. And you do not have to limit your choices to one person.

Role Models with Bipolar Disorder

A number of prominent persons have discussed their experiences with bipolar disorder. If some of these people appear to be more successful than others in their personal lives, it is also true that some have found much more success after getting diagnosed and treated. In any event, these people demonstrate that it is possible to have bipolar disorder and still achieve professional goals. Furthermore, some of their life stories are cautionary tales about what can happen to both career and personal life without treatment.

A person with bipolar disorder does not have to be famous in order to provide a good example. Perhaps in a support group or network there is someone who lives the kind of life you would like to live. This does not mean you should mimic that person, but you can apply his positive example to your life. It can pay to learn how someone you admire manages to live in a positive way.

Talk to the person about his life to learn how he deals with various kinds of situations. And if you happen to be around this person when he deals with a situation that you would find extremely difficult, notice how he handles it. For example, if he seems to manage anger in a more balanced way than you do, ask for hints about how he approaches the problem.

Role Models Without Bipolar Disorder

A person does not have to have bipolar disorder to be a role model. They can emerge from your immediate circle or they may be successful people you have only read about.

If you have a career or aspire to one, you may be able to identify someone in your field who is worthy of your respect. Even if someone is immeasurably successful compared to you, you might be able to apply something from her life to your own and adapt it to your own needs.

A happy home life does not simply appear; it takes effort. Determine what kinds of communication skills and attitudes these people have. If the people you admire are celebrities, you can at least read about them in profiles and interviews to glean hints that you can apply to your situation.

You Are Never Alone

It is not uncommon for a person to believe she is the only person who has ever felt a certain way. This especially can be the case when dealing with symptoms of a serious mental disorder. Because there is still shame and unease surrounding these issues, people often keep their fears and worries about their illnesses to themselves. But society is becoming increasingly more receptive to people being honest about their mental health problems. There are several places you can find help and someone to talk to.

For People with Bipolar Disorder

Besides the millions of people with bipolar disorder, there are many more people with other disorders and mental conditions facing challenges similar to those you face. There are also millions of people who have never been diagnosed with anything serious, but who are no strangers to depression and stress.

In Appendix B, you will find a list of organizations you can contact for support, information, and opportunities to network with people who have been through what you have been through. You also might contact your local public library or hospital or ask your doctor or therapist about groups you can investigate.

 Fact

Lizzie Simon was an honor student about to go to Columbia University at age seventeen. She had her first major bipolar episode studying abroad in Paris, but she responded immediately to lithium treatment, and has since written *Detour*, a popular book about being bipolar that led to an MTV special entitled *True Life: I'm Bipolar*.

Whatever you are going through and wherever you have been, there are people who know what it is like. Finding people who understand your experience can make an enormous difference in how you feel about yourself, how you handle your problems, and how you can build a better life.

For the Loved Ones of People with Bipolar Disorder

There is a growing understanding that bipolar disorder should be treated as a family condition. You should consider it your right and responsibility to get all the information and therapy you need to have a happy home life and feel good about yourself as you help someone with this disorder. In the end, it may help you as much as the person with bipolar disorder if you take advantage of good family therapy sessions. Learning about the illness and how it affects people can help you better cope with stress. If possible, try to engage all relevant family members in a therapeutic climate with a psychologist or psychiatrist. If some don't cooperate, include as many as are willing. If you have to, attend by yourself. You can seek out allies in support groups that a competent therapist or doctor can direct you to.

Consider networking with other people who have family members with bipolar disorder. Through support groups you can find useful information and receive a great deal of empathy from people who know what you are going through.

Symptoms Checklists

Use the following checklists for reference as you increase your understanding of the symptoms associated with different kinds of bipolar disorders. Different people have different combinations of symptoms that can change over time. Discuss any concerns and questions you have with your doctor.

Manic Episodes

- ☐ Persistent, unexplainable mood elevation
- ☐ Speech so rapid others can't follow meaning; pressure to talk; hoarseness
- ☐ Euphoria that rapidly changes to hostility or anger
- ☐ Grandiose vision of self; inflated feeling of greatness, success, power, fame, or importance
- ☐ Extreme optimism
- ☑ Denial, poor judgment, lack of introspection
- ☐ Racing thoughts
- ☐ Sleep very little but feel energized
- ☑ Physical restlessness, agitation
- ☑ Heightened perceptions
- ☑ Easily distracted; extremely short attention span
- ☑ Risk taking
- ☑ Lavish, foolish spending

☐ Exceptionally strong sex drive
☐ Substance abuse
☒ Psychosis; hallucinations, delusions, thought disorders
☐ Intense lack of inhibition

Hypomanic Episodes
(symptoms less severe than mania)

☐ Unusually high confidence
☐ Less need for sleep
☐ More talkative than usual
☒ Thoughts faster than usual
☒ More easily distracted than usual
☒ More concerned with goals than usual
☒ More inclined to take risks than usual
☐ More interested in sex than usual
☐ Other people say you are not being your usual self or not acting normally

Depressive Episodes

☒ Severe, long-lasting sense of despair, hopelessness, or emotional emptiness
☒ Wanting to stay in bed for one or more days without being physically ill
☒ Sleeping more than normal or exhausted yet unable to sleep
☒ Aches and pains with no apparent physical origin
☐ Major changes in appetite
☒ Lethargic, low energy or restlessness and agitation
☒ Lack of interest or pleasure in usual pursuits
☒ Avoiding daily responsibilities
☒ Social withdrawal
☒ Feelings of guilt or worthlessness
☐ Difficulty making decisions

- ☐ Hostile, quick to anger
- ☒ Deep, constant sadness
- ☐ Sudden outburst (such as crying) for seemingly no reason
- ☒ Inability to concentrate
- ☒ Pessimism, hopelessness, and anxiety
- ☒ Psychosis; hallucinations, delusions, thought disorders
- ☒ Suicidal thoughts or attempt

Mixed episode is characterized by simultaneous mania and depression or alternating moods during the day.

Mixed mania is characterized by episodes that consist of a blend of mania (or hypomania) and depression.

Cyclothymia

- ☒ Moods only high or low, changing for no reason
- ☒ Energy level only high or low, changing for no reason
- ☐ Thoughts either sharp or dull, changing for no reason
- ☒ Perceptions either vivid or limp, changing for no reason
- ☒ Strong emotions
- ☒ Urges to take risks or stand out
- ☒ Difficulty finishing things

Additional Resources

Organizations and Support Groups

Bipolar Significant Others
For the spouses, families, friends, and other loved ones of people with bipolar disorder.

🖱 *www.bpso.org*

Bipolar World
A source for information and support.

🖱 *www.bipolarworld.net*

Depression and Bipolar Support Alliance
A leading national organization.

🖱 *www.dbsalliance.org*

Depression-Guide.com
A resource for information about depression.

🖱 *www.depression-guide.com*

Friendship Network
A NAMI-sponsored online meeting place for people with bipolar and other disorders.

🖱 *www.friendshipnetwork.org*

Healthy Place Bipolar Community

A consumer mental health site.

🖰 *www.healthyplace.com*

Mental Health America (formerly NMHA)

This advocacy group site provides useful information about many aspects of bipolar disorder.

🖰 *www.nmha.org*

Mixed Nuts

A chat forum and source of information on bipolar and other illnesses.

🖰 *www.mixednuts.net*

The National Alliance on Mental Illness (NAMI)

NAMI claims to be "the nation's largest grassroots organization for people with mental illness and their families."

🖰 *www.nami.org*

National Institute of Mental Health (NIMH)

Offers information about mental illness and treatment.

🖰 *www.nimh.nih.gov*

Pendulum Resources

A source of information provided by a nonprofit consumer organization.

🖰 *www.pendulum.org*

Books

Andreasen, Nancy C. *The Creating Brain*. New York: The Dana Press, 2005.

Bauer, Mark S. et al. *Overcoming Bipolar Disorder, A Comprehensive Workbook for Managing Your Symptoms & Achieving Your Life Goals*. Oakland, CA: New Harbinger Publications, Inc., 2008.

Berk, Lesley et al. *Living with Bipolar.* Crows Nest, NSW: Allen and Unwin, 2008.

Duke, Patty. *Brilliant Madness: Living with Manic Depressive Illness.* New York: Bantam, 1993.

Duke, Patty. *Call Me Anna: The Autobiography of Patty Duke.* New York: Bantam, 1988.

Hinshaw, Stephen P. *The Years of Silence Are Past: My Father's Life with Bipolar Disorder.* Cambridge: Cambridge University Press, 2002.

Hornbacher, Marya. *Madness, A Bipolar Life.* Boston: Houghton Mifflin, 2008.

Jamison, Kay Redfield. *An Unquiet Mind: A Memoir of Moods and Madness.* New York: Vintage, 1997.

Jamison, Kay Redfield. *Touched with Fire: Manic Depressive Illness and the Artistic Temperament.* New York: Free Press, 1996.

Marcovitz, Hal. *Bipolar Disorders.* San Diego: Reference Point Press, 2009.

Maurer, Robert. *One Small Step Can Change Your Life, The Kaizen Way.* New York: Workman Publishing, 2004.

Perlis, Roy H., edited by Theodore A. Stern et al. *Bipolar Disorder in Massachusetts General Hospital Comprehensive Clinical Psychiatry.* Philadelphia: Mosby-Elsevier, 2008.

Torrey, E. Fuller and Michael B. Knable. *Surviving Manic Depression.* New York: Basic Books, 2002.

Index

We Have EVERYTHING® on Anything!

With more than 19 million copies sold, the Everything® series has become one of America's favorite resources for solving problems, learning new skills, and organizing lives. Our brand is not only recognizable—it's also welcomed.

The series is a hand-in-hand partner for people who are ready to tackle new subjects—like you!

For more information on the Everything® series, please visit *www.adamsmedia.com*

The Everything® list spans a wide range of subjects, with more than 500 titles covering 25 different categories:

Business	History	Reference
Careers	Home Improvement	Religion
Children's Storybooks	Everything Kids	Self-Help
Computers	Languages	Sports & Fitness
Cooking	Music	Travel
Crafts and Hobbies	New Age	Wedding
Education/Schools	Parenting	Writing
Games and Puzzles	Personal Finance	
Health	Pets	